Is the Holy Spirit for Me?

A Search for the Meaning of the Spirit in Today's Church

Harvey Floyd

Is The Holy Spirit For Me?

Copyright © 1981 by 20th Century
Christian, Inc. Nashville, TN 37204

Fourth Printing, October 1987

ISBN 0-89098-446-8

COVER: Design by Roberto Santiago - Photograph by Harold West

To Virginia
my wife
for her encouragement
and helpful suggestions

Contents

Preface

This study has two parts: (1) it is concerned with the New
Testament teaching on the person and work of the Holy Spirit, and
(2) it examines the conception of the Spirit in the charismatic
movement (both Pentecostalism and the new Pentecostalism). The
first six chapters consider who the Holy Spirit is, his chief mission,
what he does in the life of the Christian, the conditions of his
indwelling, and the evidences of his presence in the Christian's life.
The last seven chapters probe the sources from which the
charismatic movement has developed and evaluate its view of the
Spirit's activity. The Pentecostal understanding of the Spirit is
evaluated in relation to the New Testament doctrine of the Spirit,
the work of Christ, and other cardinal New Testament teachings.
The final two chapters deal with the question of miraculous gifts,
especially with the gifts most highly prized in the charismatic
movement—glossolalia and healing.

The questions in the "Questions and Answers" section at the end
of chapters have special importance. Their value lies in the fact that
they are real questions asked by thoughtful students. Most of the
questions have been asked again and again. All of them have been
asked more than once. The questions most frequently and urgently
asked are: Who is the Holy Spirit? What is he doing *today?* What
are the evidences of the Spirit's presence?

I wish to thank the students of David Lipscomb College, who are
a constant challenge to me to learn and teach, for their honest and
thoughtful questions used in this study. I am grateful also to David
Lipscomb College for providing me the grant which enabled me to
complete this book.

CHAPTER I

Who Is the Holy Spirit?
Unity and Diversity in God

Key Scriptures:

(1) *The Unity of God*	(2) *Diversity within God*	(3) *The Personality of the Spirit*
Dt. 6:4	Matt. 3:16, 17	I Cor. 2:10
Mk. 12:29	Mat. 28:19	I Cor. 12:11
James 2:19	John 1:1	Eph. 4:30
Rom. 3:30	John 14:16	
	John 17:24	
	II Cor. 13:14	

When we ask the question, Who is the Holy Spirit, we must answer in terms of a larger question: What is the nature of God? The passages listed above (a representative and not an exhaustive list) give us the basic answer to these questions. The first group of passages shows the unity of God—that there is only one God. The second group establishes the fact that there is diversity within the one God. The third group shows that the Holy Spirit is personal, not an impersonal force. These facts—the unity of God, the diversity within God, and the personality of the Spirit—are the data with which we have to deal in learning who the Holy Spirit is.

(1) The Unity of God (Dt. 6:4)

"Hear, O Israel: The Lord our God is one Lord." This is what is called the *Shema*. *Shema* is a Hebrew word which means "Hear." It is the first word from the Hebrew of this passage. In the synagogue worship the Jews recite this passage regularly. It is important in Judaism. It is very important also in Christianity.

(2) Diversity within God (Matt. 28:19, II Cor. 13:14, John 1:1, John 14:16, John 17:24, Matt. 3:16, 17)

Jesus commissioned his apostles to baptize disciples into the name of the Father, and of the Son, and of the Holy Spirit (Matt. 28:19). A relationship between the believer and God the Father, and the Son, and the Holy Spirit is established at baptism. We do not establish a relationship with God in piecemeal fashion, first with the Father, then with the Son, then with the Holy Spirit, but

1

rather with all at one time. At baptism a relationship is established with God the Father, and the Son, and the Holy Spirit. This passage says something highly significant about the nature of God. It shows there is diversity within the unity of God. God is God the Father, and God the Son, and God the Holy Spirit. Otherwise, we have the incongruous view that our relationship is said to be with the Creator and with two creatures, and the creatures are associated with the Creator by the singular name and the three are reached by one action. For the Son is either God the Son or a creature, and the Spirit is either God the Spirit or a creature. There is no middle ground.

Paul concludes the second Corinthian letter with the prayer: "the grace of the Lord Jesus Christ, and the love of God, and the communion of the Holy Spirit, be with you all" (II Cor. 13:14). Here, again, we see either diversity within God or the incompatible joining of creature with Creator. In other words, can this triad, this Trinity, be composed of a created being plus the Creator plus another created being?

"In the beginning was the Word and the Word was with God and the Word was God" (John 1:1). This is a specific statement that the diversity is a difference between persons both of whom are affirmed to be God. "I will pray the Father," said Jesus, "and he will give you another Comforter" (John 14:16). Weigh the word "another" carefully. It affirms a difference in persons between the Son and the Spirit. The fact that Jesus addresses prayer to the Father ("I will pray the Father") is significant also; it means that the Father and the Son cannot be identical persons. The fact that the Father loves the Son shows the same point (John 17:24).

At the baptism of Jesus three distinct persons are present and interacting with one another: the Father, who declares him to be his Christ, the Spirit, who comes to him symbolized by a dove, and, of course, Jesus himself, who is conscious of the Father's acknowledgment and the Spirit's coming. "And Jesus, when he was baptized, went up straightway from the water: and lo, the heavens were opened unto him, and he saw the Spirit of God descending as a dove, and coming upon him; and lo, a voice out of the heavens, saying, This is my beloved Son, in whom I am well pleased" (Matt. 3:16,17; parallels in Mk. 1:9-11, Lk. 3:21-22, John 1:32-34).

(3) The Personality of the Spirit (Eph. 4:30, I Cor. 2:10, and I Cor. 12:11)

"Grieve not the Holy Spirit of God, in whom ye were sealed unto the day of redemption" (Eph. 4:30). Do not make the Holy Spirit sad or cause sorrow to the Holy Spirit by an improper Christian walk, including such things as lying, harboring anger, stealing, and showing bitterness or malice (Eph. 4:25-31). The fact that the Holy

2

Spirit can experience sorrow shows beyond question that he is self-conscious and personal. A person is one who can think, purpose, reason, feel, know. The Holy Spirit has exhaustive knowledge, even of the "depths" of God (I Cor. 2:10). He can be neither a finite being nor the impersonal energy of God. Neither is the Spirit simply God in action, for the Spirit himself purposes (I Cor. 12:11).

The Unity of God

Now let us turn to a discussion of the unity of God. This must be the starting point for any discussion of God's nature. The fundamental statement of God's unity is Deuteronomy 6:4: "Hear O Israel, the Lord our God is one Lord." Whatever conclusions we reach about the nature of God, we must leave this passage intact. There is only one God; there are not three gods. There is not a multiplicity of gods; there is only one. This is essential not only to Judaism, but to Christianity as well. When Jesus was asked what is the first commandment in the law, he said (quoting Dt. 6:4,5): "The first is, Hear, O Israel; the Lord our God, the Lord is one: and thou shalt love the Lord thy God with all thy heart, and with all thy soul, and with all thy mind, and with all thy strength" (Mk. 12:29,30). There is one God and man shall love him with all his being. That is the first commandment—recognizing that God is one and that he is the only object worthy of our utmost devotion.

"Thou believest that God is one; thou doest well" (James 2:19). It is true, according to the book of James, that there were people who rested on this basic principle alone. It is not enough to rest on this alone, but it is primary that a person recognize the fact that there is one God. A Moslem once asked me, "Is it a Christian belief that God is one?" He thought that Christians do not believe in one God but in three. "Yes, of course, this is Christian belief," I assured him; "there is one God, not three."

In Romans 3:30 Paul is showing that there is one plan of salvation for all people. And on what does he rest this conclusion? On the fact that there is one God. There is not one plan of salvation for the Jews and another for the gentile. And why not? Because God is one. He will justify the Jew by faith and will justify the gentile in the same way, by the same faith. The fact that there is one God is essential to Christianity, and the unity of God is taught not only in the Old Testament but in the New Testament as well.

Unity in Diversity

Now that we have seen the importance of God's unity, the second point we should consider is this: what is the nature of God's unity? Is it monolithic? Monolithic is from two Greek words: *monos* and *lithos*. *Monos* means "one" and *lithos* means "stone."

3

A monolith is one big stone; it is undifferentiated; it is the same through and through. Monolithic means "without any differences." It means that there is no diversity in unity; there is only one undifferentiated mass. Is God's unity monolithic? Or is his unity complex? Is God's unity more like the unity of a living organism, like a unified body of people, or is his unity a simplistic, monolithic unity?

We find help in understanding a unity which permits diversity within itself from Jesus' prayer that all believers might be "one" (John 17:20-23). What will be the nature of their oneness? Will it be monolithic? It cannot be; it will be a unity in which there are many constituent elements. There will be one in many in this kind of unity. "That they all may be one," Jesus prayed, "even as thou, Father, art in me, and I in thee, . . . that the world may believe that thou didst send me." Now, Jesus is saying that the unity of God and himself is to be the model of the unity of his disciples.

What is the nature of the unity of his disciples? "For as the body is one, and hath many members, and all the members of the body, being many, are one body, so also is Christ" (I Cor. 12:12. In this sentence "Christ" is a metonomy for the church). The unity of the church is a complex unity; it is a unity composed of many elements. We are using this passage simply as an illustration of complex unity. Of course, God's unity is more profoundly complex than ours, but complex it is. His unity is like that of a living organism, or of a great work of art, literature, or music. There is one God, one Divine Being, but there is diversity within his oneness. God is a triad; there are three persons. This language causes us some difficulty. When we think of three persons, we tend to think of three separate beings but we must resist this tendency. Three separate beings (or gods) is not what the language is intended to convey, and more importantly, that is not the reality which lies behind the language.

God's unity is like the unity of the atom—a unity in diversity. The ancient Greeks believed the atom was indivisible. That is what the word *atom* means. *Atomos,* as Democritus called it, means something that cannot be "cut" or divided any further. That conception of the atom illustrates a very simplistic kind of unity. Democritus thought of the atom as being a kind of little pellet, a very small piece of matter of which all things are made. And the atom, he thought, could not be divided any further. We have learned that that view is incorrect; the atom can be divided and is extremely complex. The smallest thing in God's creation reflects unity in diversity. Always there has been the philosophical question, How can we account for unity in diversity? For diversity in unity? The Christian has an answer to this. The answer is found in the will of the creating God, whose own nature reflects diversity within unity.

4

Now, it is an exciting thing that this unity in diversity in God is reflected in God's creation. I remember how excited I was when I first looked into a microscope at a section of a leaf and realized that a leaf does not possess a simplistic unity. I found that the leaf was not stationary, that it has elements (chloroplasts) in it which were in motion. It was complex beyond my previous imagining.

The complexity of God's nature should not surprise us. All reality, including our own nature, is exceedingly complex. We should expect the nature of God, who is ultimate reality, to be far more complex than his creation. When we learn for the first time that God is not one person but three—Father, Son, and Holy Spirit—we are learning, not that there are three gods when we thought there was one, but only that God is much bigger than we had imagined. This fact about God—that he is one and yet exists forever in the three-fold personal relationship of Father, Son, and Holy Spirit—is what is meant by the doctrine of the Trinity.

Questions and Answers

1. Are we really expected to be able to understand the Holy Spirit?

In answering a question like this, it is imperative to understand the difference between true knowledge and total knowledge. It is possible to know something truly without knowing it perfectly or exhaustively; in fact, as finite beings we can know nothing exhaustively. Only the infinite God has complete, total knowledge. Let me give a sample illustration of the difference between true knowledge and exhaustive knowledge. Let me tell you about a book I have: it is a Greek Testament; it is a gift from the class of 1969. Now I have given you true and infallible information, but it is not exhaustive information. You could go on forever learning about the book. As to the Holy Spirit, we may know him truly; we have true information about him because it is given to us in Scripture, but we can never know him exhaustively.

2. Can we properly use the word "Trinity" since it does not occur in the Bible?

Yes, just as we may use the word "Bible" though the word does not occur in the Scriptures. The decisive questions here are: (1) is the *idea* found in the Scriptures? and (2) does the *word* proposed adequately express the idea? The idea conveyed by the word "Bible" is certainly present. The Scriptures are "the book" *par excellence*. Just so, we may use the word "Trinity," for the word adequately conveys what Scripture teaches about the nature of God.

5

3. What does it mean that the Spirit came as a dove at the baptism of Jesus?

The dove was the visible sign of the invisible Spirit, whose coming identified Jesus as the Christ (John 1:32-34). Admired for its beauty (Ps. 68:13, Song of Solomon 1:15), a symbol of hope (Gen. 8:8-11) and gentleness (Matt. 10:16), the dove was a fitting symbol of the Spirit exhibited in the disposition and manner of Jesus.

> I will put my Spirit upon him, . . .
> He shall not strive, nor cry aloud; . . .
> A bruised reed shall he not break,
> And smoking flax shall he not quench
> (Matt. 12:18-20).

Try to imagine the Spirit at work in the ministry of Jesus being represented by a bird of prey. It is incongruous. Not with fiery exuberance did Jesus come, but with gentleness, inspiring hope and bringing peace (cf. Matt. 11:28-30). Compare the symbolism of Jesus' triumphal entry into Jerusalem:

> Behold, thy King cometh unto thee,
> Meek, and riding upon an ass (Matt. 21:5).

4. How did the Holy Spirit come to be? Jesus was born; God has always been; where did the Holy Spirit come from?

Jesus' birth does not mark the beginning of his existence, but only his entrance into the world (John 1:14). He is eternal (John 1:1). Neither has the Spirit come into existence but has always been God the Spirit and always has been with God the Father and the Son. The basis for this statement is given in Chapter II. If the Spirit has come into existence, he is a creature or an impersonal force—a view which cannot be harmonized with the Biblical evidence.

5. Where is the Holy Spirit first mentioned?

In Genesis 1:2: "the Spirit of God moved upon the face of the waters."

6. How do you know there is a Holy Spirit?

We know there is a Holy Spirit because God in his great mercy has chosen to tell us what he, God, is like. The invisible attributes of God—"his everlasting power and divinity"—are discernible in the created universe (Rom. 1:20), but we could never have learned that he is a Trinity unless he had told us.

6

7. **Did the Holy Spirit work in the Old Testament the same as in the New and in these days? It seems the Holy Spirit is spoken of more in the New Testament. Why? Did those in the Old Testament know of the Holy Spirit and his nature?**

It is true that more is revealed about the Holy Spirit in the New Testament than in the Old Testament. The Old Testament, however, recognized the activity of the Holy Spirit. See, for instance, Gen. 1:2, Ex. 31:1-5, I Sam. 16:13, Is. 48:16, Zech. 4:6. Why is the Holy Spirit spoken of more in the New Testament? In the Bible truth is revealed progressively as man's capacity to grasp it is developed (cf. John 16:12). Progressive revelation is not the same as evolution of doctrine, a view which holds that there is no revelation at all but that men began with primitive ideas of God and over a long period stripped away the unworthy elements until the sublime view of one ethical God emerged. Progressive revelation, to the contrary, means that whatever is revealed at any period is infallibly true, yet not all that could be revealed is actually revealed. For example, Gen. 3:15, the first promise of the coming Messiah is infallibly true, but it leaves a great deal still to be told about the Messiah, his person and his work. Isaiah 53 is no more true than Genesis 3:15, but it is much fuller. So, while the New Testament doctrine of the Spirit is fuller, it is not more true than what is taught in the Old Testament. The Old Testament doctrine of God hammers home especially the fact that God is one and that he is a moral God.

As to whether the Holy Spirit worked in the Old Testament as in the New, see I Peter 1:10-12 and the discussion of that passage in chapter III, question 5. The Spirit worked in the prophets and in others as God willed, but he was not promised to each son and daughter of God as he is in the New Testament (John 7:37-39).

8. **Why is there such an evasion of discussing the Holy Spirit in the church or with non-Christians? The typical remark when reading something about the Holy Spirit in the Bible is "We don't want to get into that."**

Is this attitude generally prevalent? If it is present to any extent in any place on any subject, it is quite dangerous. Whenever any teaching of Scripture fails to be taught or properly emphasized in the total context of Biblical teaching, someone always comes along to rip it from its context and emphasize it apart from its Biblical perspective. Wherever the attitude asked about prevails, the reason is likely the belief that the best way to prevent errors about the Spirit is to avoid the subject altogether—a course liable to produce the very situation feared.

7

9. How does a literal meaning of John 1:1 affect our perception of it? I understand the literal meaning is "a god was the word."

It is the contention of Jehovah's Witnesses that John 1:1 should be rendered "the word was a god," because in the Greek text "God" (*theos*) here lacks the article. (The Greek language has only the definite article, *the*. Since the definite article is not used here, the Jehovah's Witnesses assume they may translate it "a god"). This rendering cannot be reconciled with monotheism. Christ cannot be "a god." According to Scripture there is only one God. All others exist only in the imaginations of men. Christ is either "God" or a false god. Aside from the doctrinal difficulties in the rendering "a god," what about the grammar? In the first eighteen verses of John "God" (*theos*) occurs at least four other times without the article (1:6, 12, 13, 18). Should we render verse 6: "There came a man sent from a god?" verse 12: "children of a god?" verse 13: "born. . . .of a god?" verse 18: "No man hath seen a god?" Such statements would be suitable in a pagan, but not a Christian, context. To be consistent the Witnesses should render *theos* in all these verses "a god." They have not done that.

Without the article the quality and character of the word "God" are stressed. It is not indefinite. The presence of the article would have particularized the word, marked it as specific. The force of John's statement is: "the word was Deity;" "Christ possessed the full nature and qualities of God."

10. Did Jesus realize he was part of the Trinity before his baptism?

It seems to me that his question at the age of twelve, "Knew ye not that I must be in my Father's house?" (Lk. 2:49), shows that he knew already. We have the statement in Luke 2:52: "Jesus advanced in wisdom and stature, and in favor with God and men." His humanity was true humanity, and therefore he could grow in his understanding as he could grow physically. I cannot tell you when in his humanity he realized who he was. He certainly knew at his baptism. In his deity, he always knew; as God, he was omniscient. In his humanity he had to learn and in his humanity there were things he did not know. He did not know the time of his second coming (Matt. 24:36). In his Godhood he knew; in his manhood he did not.

11. When Christ was on earth was there still a Trinity?

Yes, because Christ did not cease to be God the Son when he became man (John 1:1, 20:28). On this point the account of the baptism of Jesus is instructive (Matt. 3:16,17). What do we have at the baptism of Jesus? We have one person, God the Son who has

8

become man in Jesus Christ (without divesting himself of Godhood—an intrinsic impossibility). We have the voice from God the Father, saying, "This is my beloved Son, in whom I am well pleased." And we have the descent of the Holy Spirit from heaven. There are the three. The Trinity is an eternal Trinity.

12. Is the term "Godhood" synonymous with "Godhead"?

Yes, that is right. The word "head" is a qualitative suffix. The word "hood" is also a qualitative suffix, and they are synonymous, but the word "head" has almost completely dropped out of usage except in the word "Godhead." Godhead means the same thing as Godhood and it would perhaps be more meaningful to us if we used Godhood instead of Godhead. What is manhood? Manhood is all those qualities and attributes that make a man a man. Womanhood is all those qualities and attributes that make a woman a woman. Godhood is all those qualities and attributes that make God the ever blessed being we call God. In the great passage in Colossians 2:9, Paul says: "In him dwells all the fullness of Godhood bodily." That is to say he is fully or completely God. All the qualities and attributes that make God God, he possesses.

Questions to Guide Study

1. How significant in Christianity is the fact that God is one?
2. Where is the *Shema* (Dt. 6:4) quoted in the New Testament?
3. Can you give illustrations in nature of unity in diversity? In literature, art, music?
4. What passages speak of the Father, Son, and Holy Spirit in the same statement? Do you believe justice can be done to these statements if the Son and the Spirit are held to be creatures?

9

CHAPTER II

Who Is the Holy Spirit?
The Doctrine of the Trinity

In all of church history only four basic explanations have been put forward to explain the unity and diversity of God. All of the explanations can be reduced to one of the four.

Tritheism

The simplest attempt to explain the diversity of God is tritheism. Tritheism means that there are three gods. This is an alternative that some people will present to you even today. If you talk with a Mormon, for instance, about the Trinity or about the nature of God, he will say, "Oh, it's very easy; you have three gods; you have a multiplicity of gods." He does not even limit the number of gods. The Mormon truly is a polytheist, and he believes the number of gods can be increased; that if you are a Mormon you may become a god someday yourself. This explanation cannot be accepted; it is broken apart on Deuteronomy 6:4: there is one God. Tritheism gives attention only to the diversity of God and not to his unity.

Arianism

The next simplest attempt to deal with God's diversity is Arianism. This name is derived from one of the most prominent advocates of this view—Arius. He lived in the fourth century and was a church official (presbyter) in Alexandria. Arius taught that the term "begotten" used of Christ means that there was a beginning to his existence. He made up some catchy, doggerel poems and had his people sing them: "there was a time when he did not exist," and "before he was created he did not exist." According to Arius, God the Father existed from eternity; God the Son was created in time by the Father. Arius said the very fact that he is called "Son" means that he is not eternal and is less than the Father. He was brought into existence in time—he was created. The Holy Spirit, said Arius, is a creation of the Son. The Spirit thus becomes the creature of a creature. Arianism takes account, though improperly, of the diversity of God, but it limits the unity of God to a unity of purpose.

Arianism, too, will be presented to you today as a living option by some people. Jehovah's Witnesses, for example, hold this view; they are Arians. But these modern Arians go even further in reducing the Holy Spirit. They say the Holy Spirit is not personal; he is an impersonal force. They refer to the Holy Spirit as an "it," and do not capitalize the name. According to the Jehovah's Witnesses, the modern Arians, the Holy Spirit is an impersonal force which God sends into the world to accomplish his purpose. It is the power God uses to effect his will.

Sabellianism

A far more difficult and subtle explanation is Sabellianism. The name is derived from one of the most prominent advocates of this view—Sabellius—who lived in the third century. Another name for Sabellianism is modalism. Still another name for the same idea is patripassionism. Patripassionism is from the Latin word *pater,* father, and *passio,* which means suffering. This is the name given to Sabellianism by the church fathers in criticism of the view. They said that if Sabellianism is true, then when Christ suffered, the Father suffered, and when Christ died, the Father died; so they called it patripassionism, the "suffering of the Father." A more descriptive term is modalism. This view says, "It's very easy to explain the Trinity, to explain God's unity and diversity: there is one person in the Godhead." God, on this view, is one person, not one being simply, but one person, and God manifests himself to the world in three different ways or in three different modes. He plays three different roles, not simultaneously, but successively.

Modalism can best be illustrated, perhaps from ancient Greek drama. The actors in Greek drama wore masks, so that one person could play different roles. We would have an actor come out on the stage with his mask and play a part. He is one character here as he plays his role before us; then he departs. The same actor comes back wearing a different mask. He is playing a second part now, taking the role of a different character. He cannot play these roles simultaneously, but he must play them successively. He departs again and comes back with another mask. He is playing a third role now, but he is the same person; he only wears different masks and plays different roles. We could never have the three characters on the stage at the same time. According to modalism, this is the explanation for God's unity and diversity: there is one person, but he plays different roles. He now presents himself to the world as Creator, or Father, and now as Redeemer, or the Son, and now as Revealer, or the Holy Spirit; but he is only one person, not three. Sabellianism or modalism is thus seen to be pre-occupied with the unity of God and to deal inadequately with the diversity within God. Sabellianism is presented as a living option by almost all modern theology and by the "Jesus only" people (the United Pentecostal Church.)

11

The Doctrine of the Trinity

We have just one more alternative, of all the views that have been presented to the world. The only one left is the doctrine of the Trinity. The word "Trinity" is from the Latin word *trinitas,* and *trinitas* is from another Latin word, *trinus,* which means "three-fold." The word *trinitas* means a triad. It is the right word to describe the facts presented to us in Scripture. God is a triad; he is not three gods, but he is a triad. The word "triad" means "a group of three." The word is the right word because it suggests at one and the same time unity and diversity. God is a Trinity. What the doctrine of the Trinity says is that God is one God, and that is what we have to maintain according to Deuteronomy 6:4. But he exists in three persons, and he exists *eternally* in three persons—Father, Son, and Holy Spirit. He is not playing three roles one after the other, but he exists eternally and simultaneously in the three-fold relationship of Father, Son, and Holy Spirit. The unity consists, not in the unity of purpose only, but in the one common nature, in the sameness of Godhood. The diversity consists in the fact that Father, Son, and Holy Spirit are distinguishable.

The Doctrine of the Trinity Expressed in Three Statements

The doctrine of the Trinity can be stated in three propositions. First, God is one God. Second, the Son is fully God and is distinct from God the Father and God the Spirit. There is nothing in the concept God, no quality, no attribute, which the Son does not possess. Yet he is not the same person as the Father or the Spirit. The third proposition is: the Holy Spirit is fully God, is distinct from God the Father and God the Son, and is personal. The last word is essential because, though no one denies the personality of the Father or the Son, some do deny the personality of the Spirit. The Holy Spirit is not a created being or energy released into the world by God but is deity. Yet he is different in his person and different in his mission from God the Father and God the Son.

Confirmation of the Second Statement

Since the first proposition (God is one) does not need additional confirmation, we turn to the second. The distinction between Father and Son is shown in very many ways in the Scriptures. For instance, in the fact that the Son addressed his prayer to the Father (John 17). It is shown in the fact that the Father sent the Son into the world. In the simple, moving words of John 3:16: "God so loved the world, that he gave his only begotten Son, that whosoever believeth on him should not perish, but have eternal life." The distinction between the Father, the Son, and the Spirit is shown

12

conclusively in the one statement of John 14:16: "I will pray the Father, and he shall give you another Comforter." There is, then, a distinction in person and mission between Father, Son, and Spirit, and that, in addition to God's unity, is what the doctrine of the Trinity maintains.

Further confirmation of the second statement is found in John 1:1: 'In the beginning was the Word." That statement is contrary to Arianism. Arianism insists there was a time when the Son did not exist. "Word" refers not to the word written, but to the personal Word, Jesus Christ. This is apparent from John 1:14: "the Word became flesh." It is a peculiarity of John the Apostle that he refers to Jesus Christ as the Word (John 1:1,14, I John 1:1, Rev. 19:13). He means to convey the idea that Christ is the revelation of God the Father. A word is an audible or visible revelation of an invisible idea. God, like an unseen idea, is himself invisible (John 1:18, I Tim. 1:17); what he is like becomes evident in Christ. John therefore calls him the Word. The one we know as the revelation of God, the Word of God, already existed in the beginning (of creation). That means he was not created. John does not say, "In the beginning the Word came into existence" or "the Word was created." Rather, he says that when God began the work of creation, the Word existed already. He is eternal.

"And the Word was with God." In the light of this statement modalism is impossible. The word "with" implies communion, the association of persons. As literally as this can be translated, it is "the Word was face to face with God," "he was toward God" (*pros ton theon*). The Word existed in the beginning, and he was enjoying intimate communication with God. There is unity, and there is real diversity. The fact that the Word was "with God" excludes modalism. There are two actors in the drama, and they are face to face with each other. They are on the stage at the same time.

"And the Word was God." He possessed all the fullness of God-hood (Col. 2:9). That is contrary to Arianism. He was not a lesser god; he was God. All the attributes and qualities which God the Father possessed, he possessed. He was truly God, and yet he was different in his person from God the Father. So, what we have is truly one God, but we do not have a simplistic unity. What we have is the doctrine of the Trinity: that God is a triad, that God is one God indeed, but his unity is a complex unity, a unity that exists in diversity. If it is true that God exists in three persons, then John 1:1 is intelligible.

"And now, Father, glorify thou me with thine own self with the glory which I had with thee before the world was" (John 17:5). This prayer of Jesus has to be understood in the light of John 1:1. In the beginning, God the Son was with God the Father, enjoying intimate communion with him, and now, he is about to return. He prays for a return to the glory he had before the world was created.

13

In John 17:24 there is this great, significant, and exciting statement: "Thou hast loved me before the foundation of the world." Before God created other beings, did he feel isolated and lonely? There was a time when God alone existed. Everything is created except God; only God is eternal. There is a spiritual which says that when God alone existed, he was lonely, and he said, "I'm going to make me a world, because I'm lonely." Is it true that God was lonely? If you do not believe in the Trinity, you have a problem. If you believe that God is personal and that God is love, but you do not believe in the Trinity, you have a very great problem. You have a God who is finite from the start, because you have a God who needed creation. You have a God who needed to create someone he could love and with whom he could communicate. The answer is the Trinity, the Christian doctrine of God. God did not need to create; he was not lonely. There was the Trinity. God had someone to love, and he had someone with whom he could communicate. Titus 1:2 speaks of "eternal life, which God . . . promised before times eternal." To whom did he promise it? Not to men—we did not exist. The promise made "before times eternal" implies that there was communication among the persons of the Trinity.

Confirmation of the Third Statement

Once the second proposition is established, confirmation of the third is easier. The deity of the Spirit is not stated as clearly as that of the Son in a single passage such as John 1:1. It is shown rather by the divine attributes affirmed of him and by his works. The Spirit's distinctive name, the Holy Spirit, reveals his unblemished moral nature. The fact that he is the Spirit of truth (John 14:17) means that he is beyond the errors, mistakes, and limited understanding of finite beings. The Spirit is the Spirit of God. Can the Spirit of God be a creature? If it is objected that this argument is meaningless because the Spirit of God is simply God in action, the answer is that the Spirit is revealed in personal relationship with God (Rom: 8:26-27), and not simply as God at work in the world. In lying to the Holy Spirit Ananias was lying to God (Acts 5:3-4). A reasonable person could ask, "Are you sure the word God is applied to the Spirit here? May not Peter be saying that Ananias had lied to the Spirit and to God?" Yes, it is possible, but the Deity of the Spirit is still shown in the fact that he is revealed as the one who knows the heart; he knew Ananias was lying. Significant also is the fact that the Spirit can be lied to. Furthermore, the Spirit is associated with God the Father and God the Son as a Trinity (Matt. 28:19 and II Cor. 13:14). It is unthinkable that the Trinity should be composed of God the Father, God the Son, and a creature.

The fact that the Father and the Spirit are not one person, but

14

two distinct persons, is shown in the fact that the Spirit makes intercession to the Father and the Father knows the mind of the Spirit (Rom. 8:26-27). As to the Son, the Spirit is said to be "another Comforter" (John 14:16). "Another" specifically affirms that the Son and the Spirit are distinguishable. They are different, not in nature, but in their persons.

Consequence of the Doctrine of the Trinity

Sometimes we are asked, is it not true that the doctrine of the Trinity creates grave intellectual problems? The answer is no, the Trinity answers problems; it does not create them. As we have seen, it is the answer to the question: did God need to create? Do we really have a finite God who needs the creation? No, God did not need to create, because he was profoundly personal as the tri-personal God. He was not lonely. There was already love and communication before the foundation of the world. That is an exciting concept; it means that personality is at the heart of the universe. Personality has not come into being accidentally; but go back into eternity and you will find love and communication in the triune God forever. And it is this infinite God who is Creator. That is the tremendous doctrine of the being of the infinite God which is presented in the Scriptures.

Questions and Answers

1. If Christ is eternal, what does it mean that he is "begotten" (Heb. 1:5, Ps. 2:7)?

Does "begotten" mean that Christ was brought into existence, that he is not eternal, and that he is inferior to the Father, as Arius maintained? Look at the context which surrounds the statement ("I have begotten thee") in Hebrews. In verse three Christ is declared to be the exact representation of God's nature ("the very image of his substance"). How can he exactly represent God's nature if he is a creature and is inferior in his nature? Hebrews 1:6 says: "Let all the angels of God worship him." Jesus maintained that God alone is the true object of worship (Matt. 4:10, quoting Dt. 6:13). Peter rejected the worship of Cornelius (Acts 10:25,26). The angel corrected John when he fell before him to worship (Rev. 19:10, 22:9). Yet Jesus permitted himself to be worshipped (Matt. 28:9,17). He did not correct Thomas when the apostle called him "my Lord and my God" (John 20:28). According to Hebrews, further, Christ is addressed as God by the Father (1:8), is Creator (1:10), and is eternal and unchanging (1:12), a sure attribute of God (Ps. 90:2). In Acts 13:33 Paul interpreted the begetting of Christ as referring, not to a beginning in time, but to the resurrection—that is, Christ was "begotten" when God officially declared him to be the Messiah and invested him as Messiah in the resurrection.

2. What is the meaning of "firstborn" as applied to Christ (Heb. 1:6, Col. 1:15)?

We have examined the context of Hebrews 1:6 already. In view of that context, the author surely cannot mean "firstborn" in an Arian sense, for the angels of God are to worship him. In Colossians 1:15 Christ is called the "firstborn of all creation." Could this mean "first created among all (other) creatures?" We need first to determine the meaning of "firstborn." Israel is called God's firstborn son (Ex. 4:22). The first son was especially dear to the family; his brothers and sisters respected his position and authority (Gen. 37:21); he inherited twice as much as his brothers (Dt. 21:15-17). Pharaoh, therefore, should be careful how he treats Israel, God's firstborn son. God says of David:

> I also will make him my first-born,
> The highest of the kings of the earth. (Ps. 89:27).

In this parallelism "highest of the kings" explains "first-born." "Firstborn" here obviously means preeminent. In Hebrews 12:23 Christians are called "firstborn" ("firstborn" is plural). "Church of the firstborn" means that every Christian enjoys the high privilege of being "firstborn." Each Christian is equally dear to God, and each will inherit equally.

Now, let us apply what we have discovered about "firstborn" to Colossians 1:15. Does the passage mean that Christ is the first created creature (taking "of all creation" as a partitive genitive), or does it mean that he is preeminent over all creation (objective genitive)? Verse 16 gives the reason Christ is what he is said to be in verse 15. Let us try reading both suggested meanings in verse 15 and see which one the text itself supports. Christ is "the first created being in all creation," and the reason is "in him were all things created . . . and he is before all things" (v. 17). The text cannot tolerate that suggested meaning, can it? The only way it could be maintained is to falsify the text and say, "for in him were all *other* things created" (which Jehovah's Witnesses actually do). Now let us try the other possible meaning and see whether the text supports it. Christ is preeminent over all creation, "for in him were all things created . . . all things have been created through him and unto him; and he is before all things, and in him all things consist." "Firstborn" in the sense of "preeminent" is the only possible meaning sustained by the text. Christ as "firstborn" is the preeminent Lord of creation. In all things he is to be first (v. 18).

16

3. May Christ be called "God the Son" as well as the "Son of God?" Do they mean the same?

Yes, the meaning is the same. When Jesus called God his Father, his contemporaries understood that he was not asserting inferiority. They understood that in calling God "his own Father," he was "making himself equal with God" (John 5:18). Calling Christ "God the Son" is founded also on such statements as John 1:1 and John 20:28.

4. If Christ is not "younger" than the Father, why is he called "Son?"

Christ is not Son in the same sense that I am a son. I am a son in the sense that I had no existence, was begotten, and brought into existence. When God began to create, Christ already existed and was fully God (John 1:1). Nor is Christ Son in the sense of the so-called "eternal generation of the Son." No such doctrine is taught in the Scriptures. That would surely imply an inferiority in being. The title "Son" has warm, personal connotations. Applied to Christ, it indicates the relationship of love which exists between him and God the Father.

5. What is the meaning of "only begotten"?

The words are a translation of *monogenes. Monogenes* is from *monos,* "only" and *genos,* "kind," as in *homogeneous,* "of the same kind," and *homogenize,* "to make the same kind." *Monogenes* means "the only one of its kind." As applied to Christ the word means that he sustains a relationship to God which no other does. The French translation is "son Fils unique"—his only or unique Son. The word *monogenes* is used of an "only" son or daughter in Luke 7:12, 8:42, 9:38, Hebrews 11:17. It is used of Christ in John 1:14,18, 3:16, I John 4:9.

6. In view of the doctrine of the Trinity, why did Jesus say, "The Father is greater than I"? (John 14:28)

Jesus was complete in his humanity. Since we are creatures of flesh and blood, "he himself in like manner partook of the same" (Heb. 2:14), and "in all points was made like" us (Heb. 2:17). In his full identification with us he "advanced in wisdom and stature and in favor with God and men" (Lk. 2:52), was surprised (Mk. 6:6), grew tired (John 4:6), experienced the need of prayer (Heb. 5:7), faced temptation (Matt. 4:1), became hungry (Matt. 4:2) and thirsty (John 19:28), did not know the time of his second coming (Matt. 24:36), suffered and died (Heb. 5:8 and 2:14). All of these experiences refer to Jesus' state of humiliation, a state which was not his eternally, but which he assumed for our sake. Before he humbled himself to become like us, he "existed in the form of God" and possessed "equality with God" (Phil. 2:6-8). Passages which speak of Jesus' inferiority to the Father, such as John 14:28, refer to his temporary state of humiliation.

7. As to the eternity of the Trinity, are there any Scripture references to the Spirit after judgment?

The Holy Spirit is uncreated; he is God the Spirit. Therefore he does not pass away. You do not call God into being and then send him into non-being. We now have "the firstfruits of the Spirit" (Rom. 8:23). This metaphor leads us to expect a greater participation in Christian blessings in the future, including a greater participation in the Spirit. After the judgment, we shall be with God, and God, in the fullness of his being, is Father, Son, and Holy Spirit.

Questions to Guide Study

1. What views of God's nature take account of his diversity but neglect his unity?
2. What view deals with God's unity but neglects the diversity?
3. Does the doctrine of the Trinity really and adequately take seriously the teaching on God's unity and diversity?
4. Do you see the Trinity present in I Peter 1:2? in Ephesians 4:4-6?
5. Can one meet Arianism today? Or does Arianism belong only to the dead past? Can one meet a Modalist today? Where?

CHAPTER III

Jesus' Teaching on the Spirit
John 14, 15, and 16

Key Scriptures:

  John 14:16   John 15:26,27
  John 14:26   John 16:8-15

The greatest concentration of Jesus' teaching on the Holy Spirit occurs in John 14, 15, and 16. Jesus has completed his public ministry (John 12:36b), secluded himself with his apostles (Matt. 26:20), and is engaged in preparing them for his departure to the Father. He encourages and strengthens them against the approaching trauma of his crucifixion, tries to make them a unified, caring body of men, and assures them of the help of the Holy Spirit in fulfilling their mission. One point emerges as central in his teaching on the Spirit—the Christ-centeredness of the Spirit's work.

The Other Helper (John 14:16)

"I will pray the Father, and he shall give you another Comforter, that he may be with you for ever." The disciples are not told to pray for the Spirit to come. The Spirit is promised in answer to the prayer of Jesus. The Spirit is "another Comforter." "Another" implies as strongly as language can imply anything that the Spirit is not identical with Christ. "Comforter" is a translation of the word *paraklētos. Paraklētos* is from *para* (alongside), *kle* (call, as in *ekklesia),* and *tos* (an adjectival ending which makes the word the equivalent of a perfect passive participle). The anglicized word is Paraclete. Its meaning is "one called alongside" to give help. Probably the best general translation of the word is "helper." The specific help "one called alongside" might give is not indicated in the word itself. Sometimes it was used of a person who went into court to make a plea for a friend, to gain sympathy for him. The Latin equivalent of *parakletos* is *advocatus* (from *ad,* "to" and *vocatus,* "called"), from which, obviously, our word "advocate" is derived. It means one "summoned" or "called" to give help, a "friend," or "helper." *Advocatus* was sometimes used of a person who gave help in presenting a case in court or was a witness for one in court. The term, then, corresponds closely to *parakletos.*

Parakletos is used only in the following passages in the New

Testament: John 14:16,26; 15:26; 16:7 and I John 2:1. In the gospels the term is used of the Holy Spirit; in I John it refers to Christ. Christ is one "Helper"; the Holy Spirit is a "Helper" distinguishable from him. Christ helps us by pleading our case before the Father. How the Holy Spirit helps us, Jesus develops in his further references to him.

If "Comforter" is retained as a translation of *parakletos,* it would be better for us to understand it in terms of its Latin derivation. "Comforter" is from the Latin *fortis,* "strong," "powerful." *Fortifico* means to "make strong," from which comes the word "fortify." *Con (cum)* is here a strengthening prefix. *Confortare* is "to strengthen greatly." "Comfort," according to its Latin derivation, is "strengthening aid." The Constitution defines treason as "giving aid and comfort"—strengthening help—"to the enemy." Wycliffe's version of Phil. 4:13 is: "I may do all things in him that comforteth me." "Comforter" should not be understood to mean that the Spirit would assuage grief or bring cheer in sorrow, but that he would give strength and help. Though the presence of the Spirit brings enormous comfort and cheer in the midst of suffering and difficulty, these passages in John were not meant to say this.

The Spirit Comes in Christ's Name to Teach and Remind (John 14:26)

"The Comforter, even the Holy Spirit, whom the father will send in my name, he shall teach you all things, and bring to your remembrance all that I said unto you." It is a matter of great significance that the Spirit would come in the name of Christ. "In my name" is no empty formula; it indicates that the focal point of the Spirit's work is Christ. When the Spirit comes, he will bring Christ's name with him; that is the name he will speak; and under that name he will do his work. A person's name stands for who and what he is (see, e.g., Ps. 9:6; Col. 3:17). The Spirit will set forth who and what Christ is. Christ does not point away from himself and beyond himself to the Spirit. Rather, the Spirit will point away from himself to Christ. The Spirit's coming in the name of Christ means that the Spirit will represent Christ; the Spirit will not displace him.

The Spirit's mission will be one of teaching and reminding. In fulfilling their mission the apostles would need primarily two things: they would need to remember what Christ had said to them and they would need to understand what he had said to them. The Spirit will be their Helper in meeting these needs. Under the Spirit's guidance the apostles will not set off on a new course; they will be taken back to what *Jesus* had taught them (the "I" in the statement is emphatic, as indicated by the presence of *ego:* He will cause you to remember "what *I* said to you").

We may not properly take this verse as a promise made directly to us. The promise was made to men who had heard what Jesus had taught in his personal ministry. We may not, for instance, say that we are going to write a book and call upon Jesus to fulfill his promise to us to send the Teacher, the Holy Spirit, to help us. We may not expect the Spirit to help us remember the facts, give us insight into our material, and direct us in organizing it. This is precisely what Catherine Marshall LeSourd said. She planned to write a biography of her late husband, Peter Marshall. Since she did not know how to do it, she relied on the Spirit to be her teacher in creative writing. The Spirit, she said, taught her how to arrange her materials, what to include and what to leave out, how to develop the light touch, how to appeal to the emotions without being sentimental, how to use the technique of "flashback." Such a use of the passage shows no respect for the historical context of the promise of Jesus and, therefore, shows no regard for its real meaning.

Catherine Marshall said:

> So functional and effectual was the Teacher's guidance that I had fewer editorial suggestions, less outside help with *A Man Called Peter* than with any other book since, and I wrote it more swiftly.[1]

One wonders why any editorial suggestions were given or taken!

The Spirit Testifies About Christ (John 15:26,27)

"When the Comforter is come, whom I will send unto you from the Father, even the Spirit of truth, which proceedeth from the Father, he shall bear witness of me: and ye also bear witness, because ye have been with me from the beginning." "To bear witness" (*martureo*), a favorite expression of John, does not mean that one looks into his heart to find what is there and shares his warm, moving experience with others. The expression is used of testimony given in the court. It means that a person with firsthand knowledge gives testimony to objective facts—the kind of testimony that will gain a verdict in a court of law. When the Spirit bears witnesses, about what does he speak? He speaks about Christ. This is the way we recognize the Spirit of God: he testifies about Christ. He does not testify about great, thrilling experiences someone has had. We cannot recognize that someone has the Spirit of God because he tells us of his exciting, rapturous experiences. So far is the Spirit from displacing Christ or carrying men beyond him, when he testifies, it is Christ about whom he testifies.

The apostles will also bear witness, and they are qualified as witnesses because they had been with Jesus from the beginning.

21

What is the relationship between the testimony of the Holy Spirit and that of the apostles? How does the Holy Spirit give his testimony? Do we have two independent, unrelated testimonies? Or, will there be one testimony which the apostles will give with the help of the Holy Spirit, as they are guided and instructed by him? It will be the latter, will it not? Such a united testimony we see illustrated in the case of David: the Holy Spirit spoke using the mouth of David (Acts 1:16). Such statements abound in Scripture. We may read that "David himself said in the Holy Spirit" (Mk. 12:36) or that the Holy Spirit said "through the mouth of David" (Acts 4:25). Instructed by this usage in Scripture, we may say that when the apostles testified, the Spirit testified, and when the Spirit testified, he spoke through the men Jesus had chosen and prepared by their presence with him. The apostles were qualified as witnesses because they had been with Jesus from the beginning (15:27) and, beyond that, they had the help of the Spirit in remembering and understanding what Jesus had said (14:26). Jesus' words about the united testimony of men and the Spirit are echoed in Acts 5:32 ("We are witnesses of these things and so is the Holy Spirit") and Acts 15:28 ("It seemed good to the Holy Spirit, and to us").

The Convincing Ministry of the Spirit (John 16:8-11)

"And he, when he is come, will convict the world in respect of sin, and of righteousness, and of judgment: of sin, because they believe not on me; of righteousness, because I go to the Father, and ye behold me no more; of judgment, because the prince of this world hath been judged." The Spirit's work in reference to the world is a convicting or convincing ministry (*elengcho* is to "convince," "convict," or "reprove"). The Spirit convicts men of the sin of unbelief in order to bring them to faith (cf. I Cor. 14:24,25). He convicts them and brings them to faith through his testimony about Christ (John 15:26), a testimony given in the apostolic word (John 17:20). The Spirit will be engaged in convincing men of Christ's righteousness, righteousness demonstrated by the fact that Christ has gone to the Father. Though he was crucified as an evildoer (John 18:30), his death was the death of an innocent man for the sins of others. The Spirit will bring the conviction that Christ's death meant God's judgment upon evil, and was not a mere tragedy or the execution of a criminal (verse 11).

The Spirit as Guide into All the Truth (John 16:12,13)

"I have yet many things to say unto you, but ye cannot bear them now. Howbeit when he, the Spirit of truth, is come, he shall guide you into all the truth: for he shall not speak from himself; but what things soever he shall hear, these shall he speak: and he shall declare unto you the things that are to come." The Spirit will enable the apostles to understand what they cannot now grasp about the work of Christ and its implications. The Spirit's teaching will not lay a novel course but will be in harmony with Christ and be derived from him. In unfolding and safeguarding the implications of Christ's work, he will announce "things to come." This probably includes such things as the inclusion of the gentiles (Acts 10), the warning in I Tim. 4:1-5, and the teaching on Christ's second coming in II Thess. 1 and 2.

Jesus' Summary of the Spirit's Work (John 16:14,15)

"He shall glorify me: for he shall take of mine, and shall declare it unto you. All things whatsoever the Father hath are mine: therefore said I, that he taketh of mine, and shall declare it unto you." Jesus' summary of the Spirit's work is, "He shall glorify me." The emphasis in the sentence falls upon the word *me*. It is emphasized in two ways: first, the object (me) is placed before the verb (in the Greek sentence): "It is *I* whom the Spirit will glorify." Second, the emphatic form of the pronoun "me" (*eme*) is used. The Spirit of God glorifies Christ; a false spirit leads beyond Christ and has people preoccupied with some experience, some thrilling and exciting experience of the spirit himself. The Spirit of God leads precisely to Christ and glorifies him.

What does it mean to glorify Christ? Do you not agree that the task of the faithful preacher is to glorify Christ—that is, to make Christ, and not himself, the center of people's attention? Suppose someone came to a faithful preacher and said, "You are the object of my consciousness, my center of thought." Would the faithful preacher feel praised? He would feel crushed. When someone proposed to a minister of the gospel that his name be featured prominently on a sign announcing the services of the church in order to attract people, he replied, "No, put instead 'Christ and him crucified.' " The work of the Holy Spirit is analogous. His task is to glorify Christ. He does not make himself or an experience supposedly from the Spirit the focus of attention or aspiration. If the Spirit is made the object of consciousness, the Spirit of God has not been at work. Some other spirit has been active. When the Spirit of God is at work, one speaks of Christ; Christ is the object of consciousness. The Spirit of God never has people centering their interest in an experience beyond Christ.

The Testimony of the Spirit (Acts 2)

Let us now return to the question of the relationship between the testimony of the apostles and that of the Spirit. The sermon of Acts 2 is an illustration of that relationship. Peter preached about

23

"Jesus of Nazareth" (2:22), that he was crucified (23), raised from the dead, a fact supported by the Old Testament and the testimony of witnesses (24-32), and exalted to the right hand of God (33-35). The purpose of the sermon was to bring the conviction that Jesus is Lord and Christ: "Let all the house of Israel know assuredly, that God hath made him both Lord and Christ, this Jesus whom ye crucified" (36). It did bring the desired conviction: "Now when they heard this, they were pricked in their heart, and said unto Peter and the rest of the apostles, Brethren, what shall we do?" (37).

In this sermon did Peter testify of Christ? Did he convict men of sin, righteousness, and judgment? Did he bring men to faith in Christ? Did he glorify Christ? He certainly did all these things. Now, did the Holy Spirit have any part in testifying about Christ, convicting of sin, bringing to faith, and glorifying Christ? Unquestionably he did, for it was he who inspired the sermon.

The Spirit works in this way still through Scripture to convict men of sin, righteousness, and judgment and bring them to faith in Christ. The Spirit continues to speak the same message with the same meaning (cf. Heb. 3:7 and 10:15). The Spirit maintains a vital connection with the word.

Questions and Answers

1. It disturbs me that I may not take a promise of Jesus as directly applicable to me. I try to live by things I read in John 14, 15, and 16. Why is his promise not to me?

The promise of John 14:26 is *for* us, but it is not directly *to* us. The promise of teaching and reminding was made to his apostles; they alone were present during the last discourse (cf. John 13:1,2, with Matt. 26:20); his promise to them was: "He will bring to your rememberance what I said to you." The Spirit did cause the apostles to remember what Jesus had taught them. You and I have the benefit of that in holy Scripture—in the gospels, the epistles, and Revelation. Of course we may benefit from what is taught in John 14, 15, and 16. But we know, too, that we must respect the historical context of Scripture. We know that we are not told to build an ark, as Noah was, though we may profit from what Noah did. We know not to imitate Judas, though we could give spurious Biblical support for such a course: "Judas went out and hanged himself"; "Go thou and do likewise"; "What thou doest, do quickly!"

2. Is it right to call this the dispensation of the Spirit—to say that we have had three dispensations: the dispensation of the Father, the dispensation of Christ, and the dispensation of the Spirit?

24

Does this view not misunderstand the work of the Spirit? His work is not to displace Christ; it is the opposite—to glorify Christ (John 16:14). Is the Spirit willing to make himself more prominent than Christ? He will come "in my name" (John 14:26). "He will bear witness of me" (John 15:26). "He will glorify me" (John 16:14). Does this sound as if we have a dispensation of the Spirit rather than of Christ?

3. If the Spirit points away from himself to Christ, would that not mean that the Spirit is inferior?

No. It is important to understand that difference in function does not mean inferiority. The differing functions in the one body of Christ, for example, do not mean that anyone is either superior or inferior. Paul argues this point at length in I Cor. 12:12-27. Again, the fact that the wife is subject to her husband (Eph. 5:22-24) does not mean that she is inferior in her nature—lower in the scale of being. Man and woman are equal in their humanity inasmuch as both are made in the image of God (Gen. 1:27). But to be equal is not to be identical in function or in responsibility.

The Holy Spirit is content to keep himself in the background provided only Christ is glorified. It is our great selfishness which makes it difficult for us to grasp this fact.

4. What does "blasphemy of the Holy Spirit" mean (Matt. 12:30,31; Mk. 3:28-30; Lk. 12:10)? Why is it unpardonable?

If the primary work of the Spirit is to convict men of sin, righteousness, and judgment, and so to bring them to Christ (John 16:8-11), and to glorify Christ (John 16:14), what is the chief offense against the Spirit? Is it not the final and conclusive rejection of the Spirit's testimony to Christ? This is the only sin that can never be forgiven. Any sin from which people turn away is forgiven (I John 1:9), but this sin, by its very nature, is one of which people do not repent. Jesus said what he did about the blasphemy against the Spirit because men were saying, "He hath an unclean spirit" (Mark 3:30). If one makes such a statement—Jesus is not the Christ; he is a fraud—in a rash, unbelieving moment and later repents, he has not committed the unpardonable sin. But if this statement is one's final, decisive answer to Christ, there can be no forgiveness. Why? Because the only ground of forgiveness has been rejected.

I John 5:16,17 speaks to the same point. There is sin which leads inevitably to death, sin for which prayer does not avail. The sin for which intercession does not profit is the sin which refuses to confess that Jesus came "in the flesh" (I John 4:2,3). In committing this sin one is rejecting Christ's person (the Word who is made flesh,

John 1:14) and thereby his whole redemptive work. No one could reasonably expect a favorable answer to the prayer: "Lord, I know this person rejects Christ, but I ask thee to forgive him anyway."

Heb. 6:4-8 and 10:26,27, deal with the same sin. The man of Heb. 6:6 does not stumble and get up again, but he permanently falls away from Christ and *continues* to crucify (this is the force of the present Greek participle). This conduct means his rejection of the only sacrifice for sin there can be. Why is there no forgiveness for this sin? The reason is not that God is unwilling to forgive, but that the guilty person has refused to accept the only means of salvation there is.

5. What was the work of the Holy Spirit before Christ came to earth? Why has the work of the Holy Spirit changed so much?

Before Christ came, the Spirit was testifying in the prophets to Christ's suffering and the glories that should result from them (I Peter 1:11). Peter's statement agrees with Jesus' summary of the content of Scripture (Lk. 24:26,27 and 44-47). After Christ's coming the Spirit testified, in those who proclaimed the gospel, about the accomplished work of Christ (I Peter 1:12). Before the coming of Christ the Spirit spoke about what God promised to do in Christ. When Christ came, the Spirit explained what God had done in Christ and what the implications of his work were. Through Scripture the Spirit continues to give his testimony about Christ. The Holy Spirit, then, has always been engaged in glorifying Christ. Has the work of the Spirit changed drastically through all the years? On the contrary, it has remained remarkably the same.

6. Is the Holy Spirit male or female? I have heard it said that the Holy Spirit is male. Is there a verse for that?

John 14:26: When the Spirit comes, "he will teach you." See also John 15:26, 16:8, 16:13 and 14. The masculine pronoun (*ekeinos*) is used to refer to the Spirit. The feminine pronoun is never used of him.

Questions to Guide Study

1. What is the significance of the fact that the Spirit would come in the name of Christ?
2. Read John 14:16,26; 15:26; 16:7 and I John 2:1 in various translations. How is *parakletos* translated?
3. Evaluate "Comforter" as a translation of *parakletos*.

4. What is Jesus' summary of the Spirit's work? What does his summary mean?
5. How does the Spirit bring men to faith?
6. What is the New Testament conception of "witness"?

---

[1] Catherine Marshall, *Something More: In Search of a Deeper Faith* (New York: McGraw-Hill, 1974), pp. 272-273.

CHAPTER IV

How Do We Receive the Spirit?

If the Spirit of God is present with us, what is the significance of that fact? Does it mean that we are "advanced" Christians, closer to God than other Christians? If we are Christians and do not have the Spirit, what should we do? Should we seek the Spirit? How? Can we be Christians and not have the Spirit? By what means is the Spirit received? Does he come when we have met conditions beyond conversion? Or does he come when we become Christians?

The Meaning of the Indwelling Spirit: Fellowship with God (Rom. 8:9, Ps. 51:11)

"But ye are not in the flesh but in the Spirit, if so be that the Spirit of God dwelleth in you. But if any man hath not the Spirit of Christ, he is none of his." (Rom 8:9) The "Spirit of Christ" here does not mean merely the disposition or attitude of Christ: it means the same as the "Spirit of God" in his preceding statement. It means the Holy Spirit. "You are not in the flesh, but in the Spirit, if the Spirit of God dwells in you." The opposite of that statement is: "But if any man hath not the Spirit of Christ, he is none of his." Suppose the Spirit of God does not dwell in you. Are you an inferior Christian? Paul says you are not Christ's. Suppose the Spirit of God does dwell in you. Does that mean you are a superior Christian, above those "nominal" Christians? No, it does not. It means simply that you are a Christian. If you are a Christian, the Spirit of God dwells in you, not because you are a superior Christian, but just because you are a Christian. If the Spirit of God does not dwell in you, it does not mean you are an inferior Christian; it just means you are not a Christian. To be a Christian is to have the Spirit of Christ or the Spirit of God or the Holy Spirit.

In Psalm 51:11 David prayed:

> "Cast me not away from thy presence;
> And take not thy holy Spirit from me."

This is a parallelism; he is saying the same thing in different words. "Cast me not away from thy presence" means the same as "Take not thy holy Spirit from me." David had been granted the Spirit when Samuel anointed him: "Then Samuel took the horn of oil, and anointed him in the midst of his brethren: and the Spirit of

Jehovah came mightily upon David from that day forward." (I Sam. 16:13) Because of his sin with Bathsheba (II Sam. 11 and 12), he was afraid of losing fellowship with God. His prayer is that God would not depart from him. He expresses his plea in the words: "Cast me not away from thy presence." If God withdrew from him, it would mean the removal of God's Spirit. While David had fellowship with God, he had also God's Spirit. Therefore his prayer is: "And take not thy holy Spirit from me." Similar parallelism occurs in Ps. 139:7.

To possess the Spirit of God means simply that we have fellowship with God, or that God has fellowship with us in his Spirit. He is not far removed from us, but he is near us. He is present with us in his Spirit. The Spirit of God dwells in us if we belong to Christ. The meaning of the indwelling Spirit is simply this: that we have fellowship with God; that we are Christians; that God has fellowship with us in his Spirit.

The Means of the Spirit: the "Hearing of Faith" (Gal. 3:1-5)

What is the means of receiving the Spirit? If we have answered correctly the question about the significance of the indwelling Spirit, it follows that the conditions for receiving the Holy Spirit are the same as the conditions for becoming a Christian. To ask "How may I receive the Holy Spirit?" is the same as to ask "on what condition may I have fellowship with God?" Paul himself raises with the Galatians the very question that now concerns us: how, he wants them to consider, had they received the Spirit? "O foolish Galatians," he begins, "who did bewitch you, before whose eyes Jesus Christ was openly set forth crucified" (Gal. 3:1)? Perhaps someone had come to Galatia, Paul suggests, cast a spell on them and stolen away their intelligence. "This only would I learn from you" (he will ask them only one question in their present state turning as they were from the "grace of Christ" to a non-gospel). "Received ye the Spirit by the works of the law, or by the hearing of faith" (3:2)? Here are the only two alternatives we have: we receive the Spirit either by "works of law" or by the "hearing of faith."

Some people tell us that the occasion of the Spirit's coming differs from person to person. The time and conditions of his coming cannot be set down with certainty. He may come now to this man, and under different circumstances to another man, at one point in this person's development and at a quite different point in another person's life. Paul holds no such idea. He wants to know from the Galatians when they received the Spirit and on what conditions they received the Spirit. What is the means by which you Galatians received the Spirit? Did you receive the Spirit by your heroic deeds—by yielding, by absolute surrender, by laying all on the altar? Or, did you receive the Spirit by another means? Did you receive the Spirit by the "hearing of faith"?

The "hearing of faith" means that you heard the gospel and believed it; and when you heard the gospel and believed it, you received the Spirit. That is the means of receiving the Spirit. You hear the Gospel preached and believe it, and the Spirit comes. Did you receive the Spirit by doing all the law or did you simply listen to the gospel as it was proclaimed and believe it? "Are ye so foolish? *having begun* in the Spirit, are ye now perfected in the flesh?" When does the Spirit come? He comes at the beginning of the Christian's life. He does not come when you have proved worthy, after you have yielded absolutely, after you have prayed ardently enough and cleansed your heart completely to prove yourself ready to receive the Spirit. The Spirit comes in the beginning; when you become a Christian, the Spirit comes. You *begin* with the Spirit. It is not that you become a Christian, and then you say, "Now I am going to seek a second blessing, I am going to seek the Spirit. I am going to try to get him in his fulness, and when I cleanse my heart enough, desire him enough, and yield enough then I will get the Spirit." No, the Spirit does not come that way. The Spirit comes in the beginning. You begin your Christian life with the Spirit. And if the Spirit really helps us, we need him from the beginning. If we receive him after we have cleansed our hearts of all known sins by our own achievements, we have proved that we can fare quite well without him.

Understanding that you began in the Spirit, do you think, Paul asks, that you can be "perfected in the flesh"? "Are ye so foolish" (v. 3)? "Did ye suffer so many things in vain? if it be indeed in vain. He therefore that supplieth to you the Spirit, and worketh miracles among you, doeth he it by the works of the law, or by the hearing of faith" (4,5)? "Supplieth" is present tense. There is a continuing supply of the Spirit as well as the initial granting of the Spirit. "Received ye the Spirit?" refers to a past event. It implies that at a definite point they had received the Spirit. The initial granting of the Spirit occurred at the time when the Galatians became Christians. The Spirit continues to be present (continues to be given) as they continue to hear the gospel and believe it. Paul says that the way of receiving the Spirit is very, very, simple. You hear the Gospel, you believe it, and God grants you the Spirit. In other words, you become a Christian, and you receive the Spirit as a gift from God. God is now present with you in his Spirit.

This way of receiving the Spirit is so simple that it is offensive to some people. Do you recall the account we have in II Kings 5? Naaman the Syrian who was a leper came to Israel to seek healing. He went first to the king; then finally he came to Elisha. Elisha simply sent out a servant to tell him to go and dip seven times in the river Jordan. And do you remember that Naaman was offended?

Why do you think he was offended? His pride was wounded. He said, "I thought the prophet would come out and engage in a great and impressive ceremony. I thought he would call on the name of his God, wave his hands over the place, and recover the leper." As he was about to depart without being healed, his servants said, "My father, if the prophet had told you to do some great thing, you would have done it. Why don't you do this simple thing?" Finally Naaman was persuaded. He dipped seven times in the Jordan, and his flesh returned to him, as the flesh of a little child. But he had been offended by the simplicity of what the prophet told him to do.

The way we are taught to receive the Spirit is so simple that it can be offensive to us. We may say, "Well, look, that doesn't leave me anything heroic to do to gain the Spirit of God. It does not leave me any mighty work to perform to bring God's Spirit down to me." It certainly does not. You hear the gospel and believe it and God graciously grants you his Spirit. You do not win him; you receive him as a gift. That can be quite offensive to human pride.

The Means of the Spirit: Faith in Christ (John 7:37-39)

"On the last day, the great day of the feast, Jesus cried saying, If anyone thirst let him come to me and drink. He who believes in me, just as the scripture has said, rivers of living water will flow from within him. And this he said about the Spirit, whom they who believed in him were going to receive." In Jesus' day one of the impressive ceremonies of the feast of Tabernacles was the pouring of water. A priest brought water in a pitcher from the pool of Siloam and poured it out beside the altar. During the ceremony Isaiah 12:3 was sung: "Therefore with joy shall ye draw water out of the wells of salvation." The symbolic action meant thanksgiving to God because he supplied water in the wilderness and later sent rain upon the fields. Against this background Jesus spoke of providing water for thirst—the longing to be right with God—and of giving "rivers (not trickles) of living water." The figure of "rivers of water" is gathered from several passages such as Isaiah 44:3 "For I will pour water upon him that is thirsty, and streams upon the dry ground; I will pour my Spirit upon thy seed, and my blessing upon thine offspring" (see also Isaiah 55:1; 58:11). John explains that the "rivers" refers to the Holy Spirit. And what is the condition for receiving the Spirit? It is faith. Faith in whom? the Spirit? Twice in this passage we are told that the condition for receiving the Spirit is faith in Jesus Christ. It is not faith in the Spirit as the object of faith. It is simply faith in Christ, and that agrees with what Paul says in Gal: 1-5: you receive the Spirit by the "hearing of faith" and you receive him "in the beginning."

The Means of the Spirit: Baptism (Acts 2:38)

"Repent ye, and be baptized every one of you in the name of Jesus Christ unto the remission of your sins; and ye shall receive the gift of the Holy Spirit." The Holy Spirit is received at a definite time. He is received when one becomes a Christian, at the beginning of his Christian life, precisely at the point of baptism. The Spirit is received in the water of the new birth; the Spirit is received at the point of baptism; the Spirit is received by faith; the Spirit is received in the beginning (Gal. 3:1-5).

"The gift of the Holy Spirit" means the gift which is the Holy Spirit. "Of the Holy Spirit" is a defining genitive or an appositional genitive and it would be anagolous to say "the city of Athens" (polis Athenon). That is, the city which is Athens. It does not mean a gift which the Spirit gives to you. If it means a gift which the Spirit gives to you, what is that gift? Is it salvation? No, the scriptures do not teach us that salvation is a gift of the Spirit. Forgivenesss of sins? No, the scriptures do not teach us that forgiveness of sins is a gift of the Spirit. It is the gift which is the Holy Spirit, graciously given. When? At baptism. Is this contrary to what Jesus said in John 7:37-39 where He said that the condition for receiving the Spirit is faith in Him? This is a problem only if one fails to see the union of faith and baptism (see Gal. 3:26,27). The meaning of baptism is faith in Christ. Baptism is a confession of faith in Christ. It means faith; it does not mean something contrary to faith or other than faith. The Spirit's coming is by faith and his coming is precisely at the point of baptism.

The Spirit Is Given as a Refreshing Drink in Baptism (I Cor. 12:13)

"For in one Spirit were we all baptized into one body, whether Jews or Greeks, whether bond or free, and were all made to drink of one Spirit." This verse supports the statement that the church is one body composed of many members: we all, many as we are, are all members of one body. When did we become members of that one body? When we, by one Spirit were baptized into the one body. And what else happened when we were baptized into the one body? At that time we were given to drink of the one Spirit. You will notice that Paul repeats "one" three times and "all" twice. "In *one* Spirit were we *all* baptized into *one* body. . . .and were *all* made to drink of *one* Spirit."

Now, let me ask you to consider this question very seriously. In the light of Paul's statement would it be possible to believe that only some Christians, those who pressed on to a "higher experience," were given to drink of the one Spirit? Is that what Paul is saying? Is he dividing the church into "nominal" Christians and superior Christians? The nominal Christians do not have the

Spirit, or they do not have the Spirit in very great measure; they have only a trickle. But there are superior Christians who have the Spirit, or have the Spirit in greater abundance. Could we understand Paul that way? If we do, we destroy what he is trying to say. What he is saying is that the church is one body though it is composed of many members. To support that he insists that there is one experience for all Christians. "We all (without any exception) were baptized into the one body, and we all (without exception) were given to drink of one Spirit." How many Christians have received the Spirit? Every one without exception who has been baptized into the body has been given to drink of the Spirit. In Paul's bold figure, he is saying that in the water of baptism we drink in the Spirit; we receive the infilling, if you like, of the Spirit then. We receive one Spirit "in the beginning," when we become Christians.

The Means of the Spirit: The New Birth (Titus 3:4-7)

"But when the kindness of God our Savior, and his love toward man, appeared, not by works done in righteousness, which we did ourselves, but according to his mercy he saved us, through the washing of regeneration and renewing of the Holy Spirit, which he poured out upon us richly, through Jesus Christ our Savior; that, being justified by his grace, we might be made heirs according to the hope of eternal life." According to this passage, as in John 3:5, there are two elements in the new birth—water and the Spirit. God saved us "through the washing of regeneration and renewing of the Holy Spirit." The "bath" (*loutron*) of the new birth (regeneration) is also the "bath" in which we receive renewing from the Holy Spirit. Paul adds these significant words about the Spirit: "which he poured out upon us richly." When did he pour the Holy Spirit out upon us richly? He poured out the Holy Spirit upon us richly in the new birth, in the washing of regeneration when we receive renewal from the Holy Spirit. It is not true that in the new birth we do not receive the Holy Spirit at all, or receive the Spirit only in a very poor way; then, later, when we have cleansed our hearts, dedicated ourselves completely and proved to be absolutely submissive, then we *really* receive the Spirit. In the express words of Paul, the Spirit is "poured out" upon us "richly" in the new birth. This is the solid testimony of Scripture.

Questions and Answers

1. **What is there in the Greek of Acts 2:38 that is different from the Greek in John 4:10 and Ephesians 4:7?** (John 4:10: "If thou knewest the gift of God . . . " Eph. 4:7: "according to the gift of Christ. . . .") I have never heard anyone say these mean God

33

as a gift or Christ as a gift. Rather, the gift of God is obviously the living water that Jesus talks about immediately following in the passage from John, and the gift of Christ is the grace that was given as talked of in the Ephesian passage.

Your comments on John 4:10 and Ephesians 4:4 are correct. And there is no difference in the Greek construction in Acts 2:38 and these passages. The three passages use the word "gift" (*dorea*) followed by a noun in the genitive case. The genitive is capable of expressing a rather wide variety of relationships. The precise meaning in each case must be determined just as you decided the sense of John 4:10 and Ephesians 4:7—from context. As an illustration of this point, note that the Greek construction of Matthew 12:31 is identical with that used in these three passages: a noun ("blasphemy") used with another in the genitive case ("of the Spirit"). The grammar would permit the meaning "the blasphemy which the Spirit commits" (subjective genitive), but the only legitimate sense is "blasphemy against the Spirit" (objective genitive). The same construction is found also in Romans 3:22: "faith" used with "Jesus Christ" in the genitive case (translated "faith of Jesus Christ" in the King James Version). The context shows that the meaning is "faith in Christ" (faith directed to him, objective genitive) and not Christ's faith (cf. Gal. 2:20).

2. If there is no difference in the Greek in these texts, why is the gift of the Holy Spirit not the blessing of salvation that was promised to Jews and the gentiles, according to Acts 2:39?

The interpretation takes "of the Holy Spirit" as a subjective genitive: that is, the Holy Spirit as active agent bestows the gift. The grammar would permit this meaning. But it must be rejected for two reasons. First, Acts 2:38 distinguishes the blessing of salvation from the gift of the Spirit. It promises two blessings received at the same time: the forgiveness of sins *and* the gift of the Holy Spirit. Second, salvation is a gift from God, not the Spirit. The grammar will permit another interpretation: "the gift which is the Holy Spirit," or, the "Holy Spirit as a gift" (defining or appositional genitive). The meaning must be decided from the broad context of Scripture.

The Scriptures do not teach that salvation is a gift from the Spirit. Do they teach that the Spirit himself is given to the Christian? Consider these statements:

> the Holy Spirit whom God hath given to them that obey him (Acts 5:32).

> the Holy Spirit which was given unto us (Rom. 5:5)

34

Your body is a temple of the Holy Spirit which is in you, which ye have from God (I Cor. 6:19).

the Spirit of God dwelleth in you (Rom. 8:9).

the Spirit . . . dwelleth in you (Rom. 8:11).

Received ye the Spirit by the works of the law, or by the hearing of faith (Gal. 3:2)?

And because ye are sons, God sent forth the Spirit of his Son into our hearts, crying Abba, Father (Gal. 4:6).

the Spirit, which they that believe on him were to receive (John 7:39).

Salvation is not a gift from the Spirit; we receive the Spirit because we have salvation.

3. **Is there any other passage in the Bible in which there exists the same grammatical construction in the Greek as exists in Acts 2:38 ("the gift of the Holy Spirit") and in which interpreters insist that the object of the preposition "of" is the very same thing as the noun which the prepositional phrase modifies?**

There are very many such passages:

Mk. 1:28: "the region of Galilee" (= the region—namely, Galilee).

Lk. 2:41: "the feast of the passover" (= the feast which was passover).

John 2:21: "the temple of his body" (= the temple which was his body).

Acts 2:33: "the promise of the Holy Spirit" (= the promise—namely, the Holy Spirit, or the promised Holy Spirit).

Acts 4:22: "this miracle of healing" (= this miracle—namely, healing).

Acts 16:14: "the city of Thyatira" (= the city which was Thyatira).

Rom. 4:11: "the sign of circumcision" (= the sign which was circumcision).

I Cor. 1:21: "the foolishness of the preaching" (= what in the eyes of the "intellectuals" was foolishness—that is, the message preached).

I Cor. 5:8: "the leaven of malice and wickedness" (= the leaven which is malice and wickedness); "the unleavened bread of sincerity and truth" (= unleavened bread which is sincerity and truth).

II Cor. 1:22: "the earnest of the Spirit" (= the earnest, the Spirit).

Eph. 4:9: "the lower parts of the earth" (= the lower parts—that is, the earth).

Heb. 6:1: "a foundation of repentance" (= a foundation which is repentance).

II Pet. 2:6: "the cities of Sodom and Gomorrah" (= the cities, Sodom and Gomorrah).

Rev. 2:10: "the crown of life" (= the crown which is life).

The defining or appositional genitive (used in Acts 2:38 in "the gift of the Holy Spirit" and the passages cited above) is one of the most common functions of the genitive case. The usage occurs in question two above: "the blessing of salvation."

4. Does the Holy Spirit ever indwell a believer who has not been baptized in water?

In the New Testament faith and baptism are so united that the category "unbaptized believer" is unknown. See Acts 19:1-3. Paul's question to believers was not, "Have you been baptized?" but rather, "What kind of baptism did you receive?" Believers, according to Acts, were baptized at once. "The same hour of the night . . . [he] was baptized, he and all his, immediately (Acts 16:33).

5. Could someone receive the Holy Spirit if he is baptized in the name of another religion (other than the "Church of Christ")?

One is properly baptized "in the name of Jesus Christ" rather than "in the name of a religion." All who believe in Christ should be told: "Repent ye, and be baptized, every one of you in the name of Jesus Christ unto the remission of your sins: and ye shall receive the gift of the Holy Spirit" (Acts 2:38). Anywhere in the world when anyone does what Peter said, he receives the gift of the Holy Spirit and becomes a part of the people of Christ. That is the New Testament view of the church and it is totally non-sectarian.

6. If the Spirit is not given till Jesus was glorified (John 7:39), how did David have the Spirit?

In the Old Testament the Spirit was granted to certain people but was not promised to all believers. The universal promise to believers is a distinctive New Testament promise (Gal. 4:6). Before the death, resurrection, and ascension of Christ (his glorification), the Spirit had not been given as the "Spirit of promise" (= the Spirit who was promised, Eph. 1:13. Cf. Is. 32:15, 44:3) or as the "earnest of our inheritance" Eph. 1:14).

Questions to Guide Study

1. At what time in a Christian's life does he receive the Holy Spirit? What passages can you cite to support your answer?
2. How does one receive the Spirit? Are there conditions beyond conversion?
3. John 7:37-39 and Galatians 3:1-5 teach that the Spirit is received by faith in Christ. Acts 2:38 and I Corinthians 12:13 say the Spirit is received in baptism. Is there any conflict between the two statements? Why?
4. According to I Corinthians 12:13 has absolutely every Christian received the Spirit? the Jewish Christian? the Greek? the slave? the free man?

CHAPTER V

The Indwelling Spirit:
What Does the Spirit Do for Us?

What does the indwelling Spirit do for the Christian? The question is often raised: do we really need the Spirit? We have the word of God to direct us and Christ to intercede for us. What is there left for the Spirit to do? Is there any real way he can help us?

The Work of the Spirit: Sanctification (I Peter 1:1,2)

To our many-faceted salvation Father, Son, and Holy Spirit make distinctive contributions. The letter of I Peter is addressed to those who are "elect . . . according to the foreknowledge of God the Father, in sanctification of the Spirit, unto obedience and sprinkling of the blood of Jesus Christ." God chose us to be his people in accord with his foreknowledge of us "in Christ" (Eph. 1:4): that is, the election is not unconditioned. In his infinite knowledge God foresaw us as people who were "in Christ" and chose us for that reason. His purpose in electing us was two-fold: he chose us for a life of obedience and for cleansing by the blood of Christ. Further, he chose us to live our lives "in sanctification of the Spirit": in sanctification which the Spirit encourages and enables (subjective genitive). Thus in our salvation the initiative is always God the Father's (he foreknew and chose us); atonement, the ground of our cleansing from sin, is the work of Christ ("sprinkling of the blood of Jesus Christ"); sanctification is the special work of the Holy Spirit.

To sanctify (from *sanctus*, "holy," and *facere*, "to make") means primarily "to dedicate." Sanctification means that Christians are dedicated to God to be his very own people and to recognize him alone as God. This dedication occurs when one becomes a Christian, and hence is spoken of as an accomplished fact (I Cor. 1:2). It is simultaneous with justification (I Cor. 6:11). Sanctification necessarily has moral implications. One becomes like that to which he is dedicated. Hence, sanctification refers to a process in which the Christian grows in likeness to God's own character. To summarize, sanctification means (1) dedication to God (a commitment made at conversion) and (2) becoming like God in character (developing in righteousness, a process of growth never completed in this life). In a particular passage emphasis may fall either on the first or second meaning though neither is ever wholly absent. If the first meaning is emphasized, the second is understood as an obligation; if the second is stressed, the first is understood as the basis. The words "sanctify," "sanctification," "saint" (= God's person), and "holiness" are in Greek all from the same root (*hagios*). If the same English root were used throughout in translating the words, we should have "holify," "holification," "holy one," and "holiness."

The Work of the Spirit: Encouragement in Holiness (I Cor. 6:19,20)

In the context of I Cor. 6:19,20 Paul is building a case against the Christian's committing the sin of fornication. He puts forward a number of motivations which should cause the Christian to avoid this sin: (1) God is interested in the body (v. 13). It is not true to say, as some in Corinth did, that if you are a spiritual person, your body can do anything it wants to do without affecting the soul. No, God is interested in your body. And as God raised Jesus from the dead (evidence of his interest in the body) so will he also raise us, and that means our body. The body is not "the prison house of the soul" so that we rejoice when we slough it off and are free from it. Instead, it will be raised, glorified (Phil. 3:20,21), and will be with us forever. (2) Don't you know, Paul asks, that your bodies are members of Christ? If you are a Christian, don't you know that? Will you then take the members of Christ and make them members of a harlot? What a horrible idea! (v. 19) (3) Don't you know that having recourse to the harlot debases the meaning of sex (v. 16)? (4) Don't you know that the sin of fornication in a special way is a sin against your own person (v. 18)? (5) Do you not know that "your body is a temple of the Holy Spirit" who is "in you," whom you "have from God" (v. 19)? Note well that Paul's point is not: cleanse your body of its sins and, as a consequence, you will receive the Holy Spirit. The point is rather: you have the Holy Spirit already as a gift from God. Because you have the Holy Spirit, keep your body pure. (6) You have been bought with a tremendous price, so you belong to another, to Christ, who redeemed you. The conclusion is: "glorify God in your body."

There are two words in Greek for temple: one is *hieron,* which includes the entire temple area, the building plus the court (the surrounding area); the other word is *naos,* which means the "sanctuary," the building itself where God manifests his presence. It is the second of the two words which is used here. Do you not know that your body is a sanctuary of the Holy Spirit? That he is in you? What is the significance of the Holy Spirit in us? It means that we should understand this: my body is a sanctuary of the Holy Spirit: I cannot give my body over to fornication. I cannot give myself to immorality because the Holy Spirit dwells in my body. I understand I must keep my body a holy sanctuary for the indwelling of the Holy Spirit. Understanding the indwelling of the Holy Spirit is a powerful incentive for holiness. And this is why in Scripture the Holy Spirit is closely connected with our sanctification—because his presence with us is a strong motive for living a holy life.

The Work of the Spirit: Empowerment in the Warfare Against Evil (Rom. 8:13)

In Romans 6, 7, and 8 Paul is answering the question, "Shall we continue in sin that grace may abound" (Rom. 6:1)? Since we are saved by grace, may we do anything we want to do? May we say three cheers for salvation by grace and then do as we very well please? Paul answers in Romans 6 that this kind of conduct would be contrary to the meaning of our baptism, in which we die to sin and are raised again to live a new kind of life. In Chapter 8 he continues, "So then, brethren, we are debtors, not to the flesh, to live after the flesh: for if ye live after the flesh, ye must die; but if by the Spirit ye put to death the deeds of the body, ye shall live (8:12,13).

In our struggle against evil there is help for us; the indwelling Spirit supplies enabling strength. In verse 13 "put to death" is present: it implies not that we put to death the "deeds of the body" once and for all as if by a single stroke, but that it is a lifelong struggle in which we are engaged. If you are engaged in putting to death the "deeds of the body," says Paul, if you persist in that struggle with the help of the Spirit, you show that you are sons of God (8:14), and you will live. What does the indwelling Spirit do for the Christian? His presence encourges the Christian, strengthens him, and enables him in his striving against sin.

What Paul is teaching here is not quietism ("letting go and letting God"). The Spirit does not displace our own efforts. Neither do we simply grit our teeth and do it alone. "By the Spirit" we "put to death the deeds of the body." Both the "by the Spirit" and "we" should be emphasized. God's help does not diminish the need for our own effort or lessen its significance, but is rather the reason for our effort: "work out your own salvation," says Paul to the Philippians. And what encouragement do we have that we can do it? "It is God who worketh in you both to will and to work, for his good pleasure" (Phil. 2:12,13).

The Work of the Spirit: Encouragement and Help in Sanctification (I Thess. 4:1-8, II Thess. 2:13)

We receive further help in understanding sanctification and the Spirit's relationship to it from I Thess. 4:1-8. Sanctification, we learn, is what God wants in his people: "this is the will of God,

40

even your sanctification" (4:3). The content of the word sanctification is explained in the fact that it is the opposite of moral impurity: "God called us not for uncleanness, but (to live our lives) in sanctification (4:7). A specific instance of moral impurity to which sanctification is opposed is fornication: "sanctification" is to "abstain from fornication" (4:3). The second meaning of sanctification is here stressed—actual righteousness in life—though the first meaning (dedication to God) is not out of view, for righteousness in life grows out of dedication to God. Paul gives three motives for the holiness which he urges: (1) The Christian life is different from that of pagans, who do not know God (4:4-6). (2) Immorality stirs the wrath of God (4:6). (3) The Holy Spirit is present with us: "Therefore he that rejecteth, rejecteth not man, but God, who giveth his Holy Spirit unto you" (4:8). Some emphasis is placed on the word "Holy" (in the Greek text) to point up the ethical character of the Spirit. "Unto you" in the text is literally "into (eis) you," indicating not indirect object but that the Spirit actually comes into us and indwells us. What is the significance in this context of Paul's saying "God gives the Holy Spirit to you"? It points to facts we have learned already: that sanctification is the special work of the Spirit (I Peter 1:2) and that his presence is an encouragement and help in the ethical life (I Cor. 6:19, Rom. 8:13). In his second letter to these Thessalonians Paul says: "God chose you" to live your lives "in sanctification (which is prompted by) . . . the Spirit and (in) belief of the truth" (II Thess. 2:13).

In addition to encouragement and holiness, something else is essential to the life of holiness—knowledge of God's will. "Ye received of us how ye ought to walk and to please God. . . .For ye know what charge we gave you through the Lord Jesus" (I Thess. 4:1,2). The indwelling Spirit does not dispense with the need for knowledge. What shall we make then of the statement of Lietzmann: "Where life moves in the Spirit, no kind of law has any place any longer?"[1] Or of Brunner: "The believer . . . reconciled to God . . . no longer requires the Law, because God's Spirit has become the leader in him, showing him God's will?"[2] These assertions obviously fly in the face of Paul's statement: "You received from us how you ought to walk." The Spirit does not directly reveal to us the content of God's will. Knowledge of what is pleasing and displeasing to God, so indispensable for holiness, must be learned from holy Scripture (cf. I Cor. 7:19, 9:21, Rom. 8:3,4,7; 13:8-10). The Christian, filled with the Spirit, still needs the law of God to teach him the content of God's will.

The Work of the Spirit: Help in Weakness (Rom. 8:26,27)

The immediate context of Rom. 8:26,27 deals with the

Christian's condition in the present world. Verses 18-30 develop the implications of verse 17b: "if so be that we suffer with him, that we may be also glorified with him." "If we suffer with him" does not refer to enduring troubles incurred because of heroic actions on our part but to bearing up under the pervasive sense of weakness and inadequacy which presses upon us. The consciousness of weakness is present everywhere: "For we know that the whole creation groaneth and travaileth in pain together until now. And not only so, but ourselves also, who have the first-fruits of the Spirit, even we ourselves groan within ourselves, waiting for our adoption, to wit, the redemption of our body" (8:22,23). The Christian is never given so much power that he is lifted into a sense of power beyond a consciousness of weakness. The Christian has strength in the midst of conscious weakness, never beyond weakness (cf. II Cor. 12:7-10). Even Paul himself, though he had the "first-fruits of the Spirit," groaned in himself. The nature of the Christian's existence is summarized in two concepts: present suffering and future glory. The Christian at present is burdened by weakness; he looks forward to his glorification, which will place him beyond all imperfection (8:23, cf. Phil. 3:21, II Cor. 4:17, I John 3:2).

Three realities sustain the Christian in his present state: (1) He is sustained by his hope of future glory, when all the effects of redemption are perfected in him (8:24,25). (2) He has the help of the Holy Spirit in his present weakness. Particularly, the Spirit intercedes for him when the Christian does not know precisely what he needs (8:26,27). (3) He knows that God is working all things to his ultimate good. He is sure of this because he is aware of God's concern for him which stretches from God's foreknowledge of him in eternity all the way to his glorification (8:28-30).

"And in like manner [in addition to the sustaining confidence of our hope] the Spirit also helpeth our infirmity: for we know not how to pray as we ought; but the Spirit himself maketh intercession for us with groanings which cannot be uttered; and he that searcheth the hearts knoweth what is the mind of the Spirit, because he maketh intercession for the saints according to the will of God." Actually, the Spirit helps us *in* (or with reference to, dative of reference) our infirmity, as we may speak of a medicine's helping our illness when we mean that it helps us recover from the illness. The Greek word used here for "help" is picturesque. It means that the Spirit takes hold of our weakness with (*syn*) us to help us bear it. The Spirit, as it were, places himself on one end (*anti,* "opposite") of the heavy load to help us pick it up and carry it. A specific need with which the Spirit helps us is prayer. We know we need something, but we do not know exactly what. At such times the Spirit himself prays for us. Any person is fortunate who has someone who cares enough to pray for him. The Christian is encouraged and sustained by the fact that God's own Spirit values him enough to make intercession for him. The phrase "with groanings which cannot be uttered" is capable of two interpretations. The more probable meaning is the profound one that the Spirit has so identified himself and his interests with us that he "groans" or "sighs" with us since he feels our problems so deeply. An alternative explanation is that the Spirit makes intercession for us "in regard to our groanings" (dative of reference. Only we do the groaning, not the Spirit), the meaning of which we cannot express in words. On either view the passage brings tremendous assurance of God's care for us. The suggestion that the passage means that in times of stress the Spirit enables us to "speak in tongues" and gain psychological release is simply imported into the passage. That is a meaning the text does not have.

The Work of the Spirit: Assurance (Eph. 1:13,14, cf. II Cor. 1:22, 5:5)

"In whom ye also, having heard the word of the truth, the gospel of your salvation,—in whom, having also believed, ye were sealed with the Holy Spirit of promise, which is an earnest of our inheritance, unto the redemption of God's own possession, unto the praise of his glory." The two key words in this passage are "seal" and "earnest." "In Christ" and by faith ("having also believed") we were "sealed" with the promised Holy Spirit. The sign and seal of Old Testament saints was circumcision (Rom. 4:11). The seal with which God has marked Christians is the Holy Spirit. A seal is a mark of identification and authentication. A signet ring was pressed into wax on an ancient document as a sign of its genuineness. An owner of livestock "sealed" his animals by placing on them a special mark (or brand) which identified them as his property and placed them under his protection.[3] At present documents are stamped with a seal to show that they are genuine. God places upon Christians a mark to show that they are really his. That mark is the Holy Spirit, whom God promised to give to his people. "And because ye are sons, God sent forth the Spirit of his Son into our hearts, crying Abba, Father" (Gal. 4:6).

The second key word, "earnest" (*arrabon*), is a term which was used in commerce and the courts. It means a guarantee or pledge. A buyer gave the seller earnest-money—a down payment or first installment which served to bind the agreement and pledged that the rest of the payments would follow. The Spirit as the "earnest of our inheritance" means that he is God's pledge to us that God will grant us the rest of our promised inheritance, of which, in our present blessings, we have a foretaste. The indwelling Spirit, then, serves a two-fold purpose: God's giving the Spirit means that he assures us that he receives us as his own sons and daughters, and the Spirit given is his guarantee of our complete inheritance. Essentially the same great statement occurs in II Cor. 1:22 (with the addition that the Spirit as earnest is "in our hearts"): "who also sealed us, and gave us the earnest of the Spirit in our hearts" (cf. II Cor. 5:5; a similar idea is expressed by "first-fruits" in Rom. 8:23).

The Work of the Spirit: Empowerment for Life (Eph. 3:16, Rom. 15:13)

The New Testament speaks of power which is at work for and in the Christian. "I can do all things in him that strengtheneth me" (Phil. 4:13. Literally, "I have strength for all things"—all exigencies. See also Phil. 2:13, Eph. 1:19, 3:20, Col. 1:11, II Thess. 1:10, Heb. 6:5). Specific passages indicate that this power is given through the Holy Spirit. For the Ephesians Paul prays: "that he would grant you, according to the riches of his glory, that ye may be strengthened with power through his Spirit in the inward man" (Eph. 3:16). The purpose of the power given is not to enable us to do something extraordinary, sensational, or bizarre but to live life as it should be lived. Paul prays for the Colossians that they may be "strengthened with all power, according to the might of his glory" (Col. 1:11). What is the purpose of such power? It is to lead to "patience and longsuffering with joy" and thanksgiving to God for redemption in Christ (Col. 1:11,12). Paul concludes the body of the epistle to Romans with the prayer for these blessings upon his readers: "Now the God of hope fill you with all joy and peace in believing, that ye may abound in hope, in the power of the Holy Spirit" (Rom. 15:13). Joy and peace spring from faith in the glad tidings of redemption in Christ, and as joy and peace abound in the enjoyment of present Christian blessings, so does hope for their continuation in the eternal kingdom. This normal, basic Christian outlook is what is nurtured by "the power of the Holy Spirit." The concern of the Holy Spirit is to encourage and promote in the lives of people "righteousness and peace and joy." These are the qualities of life which please God and cause men to see reality and substance and beauty in Christianity. "For the kingdom of God is not eating and drinking, but righteousness and peace and joy in the Holy Spirit. For he that herein serveth Christ is well-pleasing to God, and approved of men" (Rom. 14:17,18). The power which develops these qualities is genuine power for life and service.

Questions and Answers

1. **I have difficulty reconciling the fact that Christ is our only mediator with the fact that the Spirit also makes intercession for us.**

The intercession of the Spirit does not clash with the sole mediatorship of Jesus Christ. To intercede means simply to pray for another, to implore God's help and mercy. May Christians intercede for one another? May they do so without questioning that Christ is the only mediator? Surely the answer is yes. Paul continually prayed for his fellow Christians (Phil. 1:8-11, Col. 1:9-11) and requested them to plead God's help for him (Rom. 15:30-32, Col. 4:2-4). John encourages his readers with this statement of the value of intercessory prayer: "If any man see his brother sinning a sin not unto death, he shall ask, and God will give him life for them that sin not unto death" (I John 5:16). If Christians can intercede for one another, recognizing that Christ is the only mediator, surely the Holy Spirit can make intercession for us without threatening that cardinal truth.

In I Timothy 2:5,6, the passage in which Paul states that Jesus Christ is our only mediator, he also explains what that means: Christ "gave himself a ransom for all." There is quite a difference between asking God's help for someone (the act of an intercessor) and achieving reconciliation between God and man (the work of the one mediator). Apart from the atonement, which Christ alone accomplished, there is no approach to God. In the first verse of this chapter Paul exhorts Christians to make "intercessions" (the same root that is used in Rom. 8:27) "for all men" (I Tim. 2:1). Intercession is to be made for all because God is willing to save all—a fact grounded on and exhibited by the momentous act of Christ in which "he gave himself a ransom for all."

Christ's work as mediator gained for us the right to draw near to God. The Spirit's mission is to make that fact clear, not to encroach upon it. When he intercedes for us, he does so on the basis of Christ's work.

2. Is not Romans 8:26,27 in direct contradiction to the idea that the word does whatever the Spirit is said to do? If so, how do some of our brethren deal with it?

Yes, it obviously is. Two things might be said to counter this: (1) the passage speaks of the Holy Spirit in heaven influencing God, not of the Holy Spirit in us and helping us. The context, however, deals with the indwelling Spirit (Rom. 8:9-16), and the text says the Spirit helps us in our weakness and makes intercession for us. Note in the context especially verse 11: God will make alive our mortal bodies "through his Spirit that dwelleth in" us. How could this be anything but the Spirit of God himself? (2) The Spirit is not the Holy Spirit but our own spirit. In our deep need our own spirit helps us and intercedes for us! Does our spirit stand serenely apart from us and our troubles? Scripture does not divide our "spirit" from "us" in such fashion. This conception of man is Platonic and not Biblical. Further, our spirit is not referred to as *"the* Spirit," *to penuma.* (Capitals are not used in the original to distinguish our spirit from God's Spirit. Note that the human spirit is indicated by "our spirit" in Verse 16). God knows "what is the mind of the Spirit" would be a strange way to refer to the human spirit.

3. Does the Spirit work apart and separate from the word?

"Apart and separate from the word" seems to imply that the word is left out of consideration in the Spirit's working. No opposition should be set up between word and Spirit. To dishonor the word is not to honor the Spirit. For the Spirit has spoken the word and continues to speak it every time it is read. We should think of the Spirit as really active in the word and as working in harmony with the word.

There is surely more involved in the Spirit's working than is conceived in this illustration: if I read a letter written by Abraham Lincoln and my attitude and values are shaped by it, I am being influenced by the spirit of Lincoln, and could be said to have the spirit of Lincoln. "Spirit" in such a use means no more than "attitude," "outlook," or "mind-set." There is no conception of a personal, living, and active Spirit.

The Spirit of God is really present and active in the world. He does not work in opposition to the word or leave the word behind in his working. On the other hand, it is incorrect to say that the word does everything the Spirit does or that the Spirit works only through the word. The Spirit works only in conjunction with the word.

4. If someone is not aware of some Biblical teaching or holds to some error, may we rely on the Spirit to guide him into all truth?

Apollos did not understand Christian baptism. Aquila and Priscilla did not say, "Just leave him alone; the Spirit will guide him into all truth." Instead, they thoughtfully invited him into their home and taught him the way of the Lord more accurately (Acts 18:24-26).

5. Does the Spirit make it possible for us to understand the Bible? Can we understand the Bible without the Spirit?

We should not approach Scripture with arrogance, but in humility and with prayer for God's help in understanding it. At the same time we should exert our own efforts to understand Scripture and should use proper means, such as studying in context. Prayer to understand should not be substituted for our own careful efforts. We should approach Scripture with the view that it is the

46

word of God; that it is essentially clear; that it can be understood by the ordinary person. Scripture can be understood because its central message is clear (though admittedly there are difficult passages) and because man is made in the image of God. Understanding is possible, not because of the "illumination of the Spirit," but because of the image of God in man. Paul preached expecting people to be able to understand his message. We should approach Scripture with the realization that it can be understood, as the Bereans did (Acts 17:10,11).

Questions to Guide Study

1. Does the presence of someone you respect, whom you believe to be a good person, encourage you to be better? If anyone believes the Holy Spirit is present to encourage and help, do you believe that would motivate him to do good?
2. Does the presence of the indwelling Spirit mean there is no need to learn the will of God? Cite specific passages of Scripture which bear on your answer.
3. What is the meaning of sanctification? What motives to sanctification does Paul urge?
4. What is the meaning of "seal" and "earnest"? Read Ephesians 1:13,14, II Corinthians 1:22, and 5:5 in various translations. Do they clarify the meaning?
5. What is the nature of Christian existence in this world? How does the Holy Spirit help?
6. What view of the body did the Corinthians hold? How did this affect their view of conduct?
7. What kind of life is the power of the Holy Spirit concerned with promoting and developing?
8. What is the work of the Holy Spirit now that the inspired word is here?

---

[1] H. Lietzmann, *An die Romer,* p. 71, cited in Herman Ridderbos, *Paul: An Outline of His Theology,* tr. John Richard DeWitt (Grand Rapids: Eerdmans, 1975), p. 283.
[2] E. Brunner, The Letter to the Romans, p. 141, cited in Ridderbos, p. 383.
[3] William F. Arndt and F. Wilbur Gingrich, *A Greek-English Lexicon of the New Testament and Other Early Christian Literature* (Chicago: University of Chicago Press, 1950), p. 804.

CHAPTER VI

Evidences of the Spirit:
How Do We Know We Have the Spirit?

Perhaps the two questions asked most often about the Spirit are: first, What does the Spirit do in my life? and, second, How may I know that I have the Spirit? or What are the specific indications of the Spirit's indwelling? Our present purpose is to seek an answer to the second question. What, indeed, is the New Testament evidence of the indwelling Spirit?

Some argue strenuously that only an extraordinary physical manifestation can satisfy a person's need to know that he has received the Spirit. Any other kind of evidence is called a "take-it-by-faith-believe-you-have-it-and-go-on-experience."[1] Donald Gee expresses this view:

> A weak human vessel is being filled with a divine fulness. To tell us, as some wish to tell us, that such an experience can be received without any emotional manifestation is to do violence to all sense of reality. With all due respect we refuse to be satisfied that so-called 'Pentecostal' experiences without a physical manifestation are valid according to the scriptural pattern or even common logic.[2]

According to this conception, when anyone receives the Spirit, his experience should compare favorably with the following:

> Directly, there came into my hands a strange feeling, and it came on down to the middle of my arms and began to surge! It was like a thousand—like ten thousand—then a million volts of electricity. It began to shake my hands and to pull my hands. I could hear, as it were, a zooming sound of the power. It pulled my hands higher and held them there as though God took them in His. There came a voice in my soul that said, "Lay these hands on the sick and I will heal them!" . . . In an air-conditioned room, with my hands lifted . . . and my heart reaching up for my God, there came the hot, molten lava of His love. It poured in like a stream from Heaven and I was lifted up out of myself. I spoke in a language I could not understand for about two hours. My body perspired as though I was in a steambath: the Baptism of Fire![3]

48

Sometimes the testimonies speak of outward signs observable by others as well as an internal feeling:

> When they were praying, the doctor's wife saw *a crown of fire* over my head and *a cloven tongue as of fire* in front of the crown. Compare Acts 2:3-4. The brother from Norway, and others, saw this supernatural highly red light. *The very same moment, my being was filled with light and an indescribable power, and I began to speak in a foreign language* as loudly as I could.''[4]

Often the testimonies seem to present the Holy Spirit in terms of physical energy, and a person knows he has received the Spirit directly just as if he had hold of a live electrical wire:

> The Holy Spirit came in like a torrent, as though He would tear my body to pieces.[5]

> Sometimes a wonderful shaking takes place. . . .When the Holy Ghost comes in, you will know it, for he will be in your *very flesh.*[6]

In like manner an experientialist tells us that we know we are saved when we have the experience in our souls of being saved. He asks us, "How do you know when your headache is gone? Do you know because you have followed the written directions on the aspirin bottle? Of course not. You know because you feel it is gone. In the same way you know you are saved." Then, on this view, when we feel elated, are we saved and on those days when our world has turned gloomy, are we unsaved? How dreadful to be at the mercy of our feelings! Surely we need better evidence than that. And the better evidence is that the word of God tells us at what point he forgives us. With that evidence we can reassure our hearts when we feel dejected. Perhaps you will object that forgiveness and the indwelling Spirit are not parallel. "Forgiveness," you might (rightly) say, "is something that takes place outside of us in the consciousness of God. We can know he has forgiven us only if he tells us. If the Spirit comes, that is a different manner; if he comes and dwells within us, we should know it directly." But how do we know this about the Spirit's coming? We are prejudging how it must be. It amounts to no more than saying, "It seems to me that it ought to be this way." Again, we need real evidence, evidence which cannot be readily falsified or so easily misleading as our feelings. We need clear guidance from Scripture in the matter. Now, what are the Biblical evidences that one has the Spirit?

If what we have said already about the meaning of the indwelling Spirit and the conditions for receiving the Spirit is true, then the evidence that one has the Spirit is identical to the evidence that one is a Christian. If it is true that the indwelling Spirit means that a person is a Christian, not a superior Christian, but simply a Christian; if it is a fact that every Christian has the Spirit (Rom. 8:9) and that every Christian receives the Spirit "in the beginning" (Gal. 3:3) when he becomes a Christian, then it follows that the very same evidence which shows that a person is a Christian shows also that he has the Spirit. What is the evidence that one has the Spirit of God? It is the same evidence that one is a Christian. The evidence that one is a Christian is that he believes in Christ, that he has been baptized into Christ, and that he is living the Christian life. If that is true of a person, we say he is a Christian. If that is true of a person, we should say also that he has the Spirit of God. The evidence is identical.

Evidence of the Spirit: Faith in Christ (Gal. 3:2,3,5, 3:14; John 7:38,39; I Cor. 12:3)

We receive the Spirit initially by hearing the gospel and believing it (Gal. 3:2). We thus begin our Christian life with the Spirit (Gal. 3:3). God continues to supply to us the Spirit as we continue to hear the gospel and continue to believe it (Gal. 3:5). "In Jesus Christ" we receive the Spirit who was promised to us "by faith" (Gal. 3:14). "He that believeth on me," said Jesus, "as the scripture hath said, from within him shall flow rivers of living water" (John 7:38). John explains: "But this spake he of the Spirit, which they that believed on him were to receive" (7:39). If the Spirit comes when faith is present, then the presence of faith means the presence of the Spirit. Faith itself is evidence of the Spirit. "No man can say, Jesus is Lord, but in the Holy Spirit" (I Cor. 12:3).

Evidence of the Spirit: Baptism into Christ (Acts 2:38, I Cor. 12:13, Titus 3:5,6)

If a person has confidence in the promise of God that sins are forgiven in baptism, his baptism is an occasion for rejoicing that his guilt has been removed (Acts 8:39). His baptism is evidence to him that he has been forgiven. Just so, his baptism is evidence that he has received the Spirit. "Have I really been forgiven?" the uneasy man may ask himself. "Am I sure I believe deeply enough or repented profoundly enough?" These are improper questions. The New Testament does not invite one to ask them. "Yes," he may confidently say, "I am sure I have been forgiven because God washed away my sins in baptism" (Acts 22:16). "Am I sure I received the Spirit? Did I pray earnestly enough and desire him ardently enough?" "Yes, I am sure I have received the Spirit," the anxious person may reassure himself. "Not because I was ardent enough, but according to his gracious promise, God gave me the Spirit in baptism (Acts 2:38, I Cor. 12:13, Titus 3:5,6). I am as sure

50

of the Spirit's coming as I am of my forgiveness." Is that a "vague 'taking by faith' "? Is the promise of God vague?[7]

Some have suggested that it is indeed vague. "You will receive the gift of the Holy Spirit" (Acts 2:38), a promise expressed in the future tense, is said to mean that not *in* but *after* baptism the Spirit is received; sometime in the future, perhaps months or even years later, the Spirit would perhaps be given, provided conditions beyond conversion were met. Is that interpreting Scripture according to its own intention? "Believe on the Lord Jesus," Paul said to the inquiring jailor, "and thou shalt be saved" (Acts 16:31). Could we properly say Paul meant that at an indefinite time in the future, perhaps years after believing, they would perhaps be saved? No, he means that they would be saved when they believed. "If thou shalt confess with thy mouth Jesus as Lord, and shalt believe in thy heart that God raised him from the dead, thou shalt be saved" (Rom. 10:9). Surely no one thinks the future tense here means that the salvation is to be expected at some indefinite time after the confessing and believing. Salvation is given rather when one confesses and believes. "You will receive the gift of the Holy Spirit" means "you will receive the gift" when you are baptized. The words do not place the reception into some vague future beyond baptism.

Evidence of the Spirit: Assurance of the Love of God (Rom. 5:5)

"And hope putteth not to shame; because the love of God hath been shed abroad in our hearts through the Holy Spirit which was given unto us." Paul is showing that our hope has a firm basis. Standing under it as a firm support is the certainty of God's love for us. The Holy Spirit brings us to a consciousness of God's love through the word of God:

> For while we were yet weak, in due season Christ died for the ungodly. For scarcely for a righteous man will one die; for peradventure for the good man some one would even dare to die. But God commendeth his own love toward us, in that, while we were yet sinners, Christ died for us (Rom. 5:6-8).

We come to assurance of the love of God through our knowledge and understanding of the content of the gospel. We do not know the love of God apart from the gospel and our thought about its meaning and faith in its reality. We look at the cross and reason thus: "Christ died for me while I was without strength and hopeless. That means God loves me." We think about it and say: "It would be hard to find someone to die for a good man. Perhaps someone would, but Christ died for me when I was neither righteous nor good. I am sure of God's love." This is the work of

51

the Holy Spirit, who was given to us, Paul says. What is the evidence, then, that the Spirit has worked in me and is present in my life? It is a sense of the love of God. Can a marvelous flight off into ecstasy or fantasy be more assuring than this?

Evidence of the Spirit: Obedience to God (Acts 5:32)

"And we are witnesses of these things; and so is the Holy Spirit, whom God hath given to them that obey him." The tenses should be carefully analyzed. "God hath given" (or "gave," *edoken,* aorist, a past tense) the Holy Spirit "to them that obey (a present participle, indicating a continuing action) him." In the past God gave the Spirit to those who are obeying him. He gave in the past the Holy Spirit to whom? To the people of God who now are obeying him. What is the evidence that you have the Spirit of God? The evidence is that you are obeying God. Who has the Spirit of God? The people who are obeying God. The evidence of the Spirit is obedience to God. This passage does not intend to name the condition for receiving the Spirit; rather, it means to give evidence that the Spirit has been received. The question considered here is, Who has the Spirit?, rather than How may one receive the Spirit? The passage does not say: He has given the Spirit to those who *obeyed* him. This would make the obedience prior to the giving of the Spirit. Neither does it say: He will give the Spirit to those who obey (or will obey) him. But rather: He has given the Spirit to those who obey him—making the obedience the manifestation of the Spirit's presence.

The context of this statement is that the apostle Peter is defending himself and the other apostles against the charge of disobeying the Sanhedrin. They had been ordered not to teach in the name of Christ. In their defense the apostles maintained that they were obeying God rather than men. Then they set before the council the facts of the resurrection and ascension of Christ. They back up these facts by reminding that "We are witnesses of these things" and, further, "so is the Holy Spirit." With whom is the Spirit present? With the members of the Sanhedrin, who are disobeying God in forbidding the preaching of Christ, or with the apostles, who are obeying him in proclaiming Christ? The purpose of the apostles' statement "whom God hath given to them that obey him" is to affirm that their testimony to Christ is reinforced by that of the Holy Spirit. Who has the Spirit? Those who are obeying God. The words "to them that obey him" indicate that it is the apostles, not the Sanhedrin, who have the Spirit. However, it is not the apostles only who have the Spirit. He has been given "to *them* (not *us* only) that obey him." The statement gives the comprehensive evidence of the presence of God's Spirit.

Evidence of the Spirit: The Aspiration for Holiness (I Cor. 6:19,20, Rom. 8:5-9)

The aspiration to be holy, to glorify God in one's person, is evidence of the Spirit, whose presence is an incentive to holiness (I Cor. 6:19,20). Anyone who has the Spirit has the "mind of the Spirit"—that is, thinks as the Spirit thinks and values things as the Spirit values them. (Rom. 8:5,6). Those who are "after the flesh" (who live as they are incited by their sinful nature) have the "mind of the flesh" (an outlook and a set of values inspired by their sinful nature). The "mind of the flesh" manifests itself in enmity against God, as shown in hostility to the law of God: "the mind of the flesh is enmity against God; for it is not subject to the law of God" (Rom. 8:7). The opposite mind-set, the "mind of the Spirit," is the desire to please God in keeping the law of God: "They that are in the flesh (who live their lives as they are stimulated by a sinful nature) cannot please God. But ye are not in the flesh (controlled by a sinful nature) but in the Spirit (influenced and directed by the Spirit) if so be that the Spirit of God dwelleth in you. But if any man hath not the Spirit of Christ, he is none of his" (Rom. 8:8,9). If one has the "mind of the Spirit" or (what amounts to the same thing) the "Spirit of Christ," he desires to be submissive to God. If one does not have such an aspiration, he shows that he does not have Christ's Spirit and is therefore not Christ's. It follows, positively, that the desire to please God shows the presence of the Spirit of God.

Evidence of the Spirit: The Struggle against Sin (Rom. 8:13,14)

The Spirit empowers the Christian in his struggle to "put to death the deeds of the body" (Rom. 8:13). Those who are putting to death the "deeds of the body" will live because they (only) are the sons of God: "As many as are led by the Spirit of God, these are sons of God" (8:14). Being led by the Spirit means putting to death the "deeds of the body"—warring against our sinful inclinations. Only those engaged in the ethical struggle have reason to believe they are sons. Putting to death the "deeds of the body," then, is evidence of sonship; it is at the same time evidence that one has the Spirit inasmuch as one "put[s] to death the deeds of the body" with the help of the Spirit and shows thereby that he is being led by the Spirit.

Evidence of the Spirit: The Fruit of the Spirit (Gal. 5:22,23)

The fruit of the Spirit is the characteristics in life which result from the influence of the Spirit. The qualities are the harvest which the Spirit gives because he encourages and enables the development of them. The nine qualities form three triads: (1) a description of the Christian heart—"love, joy, peace," qualities which color the whole of one's outlook and life. The Christian is not hostile, cynical, gloomy, sullen, cross, and unpleasant. (2) Characteristics of the Christian disposition, which controls one's treatment of others—"long-suffering, kindness, goodness." (3) Sentinels of conduct and character, principles which direct the Christian's conduct and relationships—"faithfulness, meekness (gentleness), self-control." If one wants to manifest the presence of God's Spirit, he should concentrate on developing these qualities. The presence of God's Spirit is shown not in spectacular feats of power, in floating up to heaven, in rapture, or ecstasy, but in the development of these simple but profoundly meaningful virtues.

Conclusion

We have found that the evidences of the indwelling Spirit are indirect. The Spirit's presence is known through the presence of the means of the Spirit (faith in Christ, baptism into Christ) and of the works which he encourages and enables (obedience to God, the aspiration for holiness, the struggle against evil in one's life, and the fruit of the Spirit). This kind of evidence for the gift of the Spirit is in profound harmony with the Spirit's fundamental purpose—to glorify Christ. The Spirit, therefore, does not make people conscious of himself but of Christ.

Questions and Answers

1. How can one distinguish between the Holy Spirit and an evil spirit?

The Holy Spirit is not distinguished from an evil spirit by the intensity of the emotional experience which a spirit may bring or by how well or enthusiastic one is made to feel. Two tests are given in I John 4:1-6. First, the Spirit of God brings true doctrine about Christ: "Hereby know ye the Spirit of God: every spirit that confesseth that Jesus Christ is come in the flesh is of God" (4:2). Second, the true Spirit is distinguished from the false spirit by the fact that the true Spirit causes one to listen to the revealed word of God: "He that knoweth God heareth us; he who is not of God heareth us not. By this we know . . . "(4:6). What is the identity of the "us" to whom we are to listen? It cannot be Christians generally because the "we" is distinguished from them; "ye" of verse 4 refers to Christians ("Ye are of God, my little children"). "We" is distinguished also from "they" of verse 5, which refers to the false prophet. The "we" of verse 6, then, refers to John and his fellow apostles, God's authoritative spokesmen. The meaning of this test for our day is that the true Spirit leads one to listen to Scripture (cf. I Cor. 14:37).

Similar teaching is given in Deuteronomy 13:1-5. Even if the prophet gives a sign which comes to pass, he is not proved thereby to be a true prophet. The ultimate test is whether the message of the prophet agrees with the revealed will of God. A negative test is given in Dt. 18:21,22: if a prophet gives a sign which does not come to pass, that prophet is not from God.

The Holy Spirit glorifies Christ (John 16:14), not himself or an experience which he brings, and promotes the doing of God's will.

2. Can a person receive the Holy Spirit even if he does not realize the Spirit is given in baptism? Can he be of any help to us if we do not even know he is there? Is it possible to receive the Holy Spirit and not know it?

Yes. Fortunately for us God can work even when we are ignorant. The condition for receiving the Spirit is not the realization that the Spirit is given, or even faith in the Spirit himself as a separate object of faith (John 7:38,39). The apostle said: "Be baptized . . . and ye shall receive the gift of the Holy Spirit" (Acts 2:38). Sometimes people need to be reminded that they have received the Spirit and of what his presence means: "Know ye not that your body is a temple of the Holy Spirit which is in you, which ye have from God? . . . glorify God therefore in your body" (I Cor. 6:19,20).

The Spirit can act for us even if we are unaware of it. Of course, we shall be poorer if we do not know about it. We shall fail to recognize some of God's rich provisions and evidences of his gracious care for us. Being ignorant of this blessing, we cannot realize how wealthy we are in Christ.

3. What is the "witness of the Spirit" (Rom. 8:16)?

The "witness' is not a warm glow in the heart or a speaking of the Spirit within a person. The meaning of the passage is made clear in the Revised Standard Version: "When we cry, 'Abba! Father!' it is the Spirit himself bearing witness with our spirit that we are children of God." The filial attitude toward God is evidence of our sonship and is the Spirit's testimony that we are sons. This interpretation agrees with the flow of thought in the context. Who are the sons of God? Those who are being led by the Spirit are sons (8:14). Being led by the Spirit does not mean that he is whispering in our ear; it means that we are putting to death the "deeds of the body" (8:13). Those who are children of God show it by the difference it makes in their lives. The children of God love God as children love their father, and they call him "Father, dear Father" (the meaning of Abba Father). Not only in their prayers do they approach him as "dear Father," but in the whole of their lives they demonstrate this attitude of love and reverence toward God. This very attitude toward God, which the Spirit has enabled us to have, is the Spirit's testimony that we are the children of God.

4. Is this interpretation of the "witness of the Spirit" not mystical?

No. True mysticism is a non-rational experience. The Spirit does not cause us to know that we are children of God in an ineffable experience. The Spirit's testimony is given indirectly in our lives, in the grateful and adoring love we bring to God, and because of which we desire to please him as our "dear Father."

Questions to Guide Study

1. Does the fact that the future tense is used in Acts 2:38 ("you will receive the gift of the Holy Spirit") mean that the Spirit will be received perhaps a long time after baptism? Why?
2. Why are the qualities of the Christian life named in Galatians 5:22,23 called the "fruit of the Spirit?" What are those qualities? What do they mean?
3. Is the Spirit of God to be identified only (or even primarily) with the spectacular and extraordinary? Can the Spirit be seen in one's daily, worthy walk before God?
4. Acts 8:26-39 gives an account of the conversion of the Ethiopian eunuch. Do you think he received the gift of the Holy Spirit? Why?

[1] Aimee Semple McPherson, *This Is That: Personal Experiences, Sermons and Writings,* (Los Angeles: Echo Park Evangelistic Association, Inc., 1923), p. 713, cited in Frederick Dale Bruner, *A Theology of the Holy Spirit: The Pentecostal Experience and the New Testament Witness* (Grand Rapids: Eerdmans, 1970), p. 109.
[2] Donald Gee (ed.), *Pentecostal World Conference Messages: Preached at the Fifth Triennial Pentecostal World Conference, Toronto, Canada, 1958* (Toronto: Full Gospel Publishing House, 1958), p. 48, cited in Bruner, p. 53.
[3] John H. Osteen, "Pentecost Is Not A Denomination: It Is An Experience," *Full Gospel Business Men's Voice,* 8 (June 1960), 7-9, cited in Bruner, p. 127.
[4] Thomas Ball Barratt, *When the Fire Fell and an Outline of My Life* (Oslo: Alfons Hansen and Sonner, 1927), p. 130, cited in Bruner, p. 124. (The emphasis is Barratt's).
[5] McPherson, p. 217, cited in Bruner, p. 126.
[6] Barratt, p. 109, cited in Bruner, p. 100. (The emphasis is Barratt's).
[7] Gee, *Pentecost,* No. 34 (Dec. 1955), p. 10, cited in Bruner, p. 84.

CHAPTER VII

The Background of Pentecostalism: Wesleyan Perfectionism

Pentecostalism is Wesleyan perfectionism taken to its logical consequences. Vinson Synan, who calls himself "a born pentecostal, trained in the holiness tradition," in his history of Pentecostalism, says: "The overriding thesis of this work is that the historical and doctrinal lineage of American pentecostalism is to be found in the Wesleyan tradition."[1] John Wesley (1703-1791), he says again, the "founder of Methodism, was also the spiritual and intellectual father of the modern holiness and pentecostal movements" which "issued from Methodism."[2]

Perfectionism was primary in Wesley's teaching. Wesley himself said that he had one chief thing to preach, and that was his doctrine of entire sanctification (perfection). This is the central doctrine, he said not long before his death, "which God has lodged with the people called Methodists" and to spread this teaching appears to be the reason he has "raised us up."[3]

The Biblical doctrine of sanctification is one's consecration to the Lord which comes with his conversion. The consequence is aspiration to holiness and growth in holiness throughout one's whole life. Because one is engaged to be the Lord's and is his, one longs for holiness and struggles to be holy. One expects that his sanctification will become entire only at his glorification. When Christ returns and raises him from the dead, transforms his humble body and makes it like Christ's glorious body, he will then be perfected in holiness (Phil. 3:20,21, I John 3:2).

Wesley held a peculiar doctrine of sanctification. Four points characterize his conception:

(1) Sanctification is subsequent to conversion or justification.

This means that Wesley is breaking apart justification and sanctification. He is saying that conversion leaves one an incomplete Christian. Wesley sees salvation, not as a single whole, but as divided into separate parts to be obtained at different moments by separate acts of faith. Everything else in Wesley's system is built upon the initial fragmenting of salvation. Without this, Wesleyanism could not exist; and without this, Pentecostalism could never have developed. Wesley says:

> Neither dare we affirm, as some have done, that all this salvation is given at once . . . we do not know a single instance, in any place, of a person's receiving, in one and the same moment, remission of sins, the abiding witness of the Spirit, and a new, a clean heart.[4]

> I believe justification to be wholly distinct from sanctification, and necessarily antecedent to it.[5]

Scripture presents justification and sanctification as inherently joined. They are two distinguishable but inseparable parts of one organic whole. Along with justification a person receives also the incentive to holiness. Sanctification is present because justification is present; the relationship is like that between fire and heat. "Can I talk of a fire that has been burning for years but only to-day gives out warmth?"[6] We cannot separate justification and sanctification any more than we can divide Christ, accepting him now as Savior and later as Lord. Paul's purpose in the whole of Romans 6 is to demonstrate that the two things are intrinsically related.

> are ye ignorant that all we who were baptized into Christ Jesus were baptized into his death? We were buried therefore with him through baptism into death: that like as Christ was raised from the dead through the glory of the Father, so we also might walk in newness of life (Rom. 6:3,4).

The idea is expressed with equal force in Ephesians 2:10:

> we are . . . created in Christ Jesus for good works.

and in I Corinthians 6:11:

> but ye were washed, but ye were sanctified, but ye were justified in the name of the Lord Jesus Christ, and in the Spirit of our God.

(2) Sanctification is an "infinitely" higher experience.

Wesley not only rends the two apart; he also lifts sanctification above justification.

> Nor does anything under heaven more quicken the desires of those who are justified, than to converse with those whom they believe to have experienced a still higher salvation. This places that salvation full in their view, and increases their hunger and thirst after it.[7]

When the body dies, said Wesley, that is an experience "infinitely greater" than any one has experienced before. One cannot imagine what it is like until he experiences it;

> so the change wrought when the soul dies to sin is of a

different kind, and infinitely greater than any before, and than any can conceive till he experiences it.[8]

Now, what, in the Biblican presentation, is justification? Justification is a legal term. It means that we go into the courtroom and stand before the Supreme Judge of the universe. The Judge pronounces our guilt removed, and we stand in the clear before God. Our sins are forgiven and we are granted a right relationship with God. What can be placed above that? If we are sons and daughters of God, what blessing can possibly be greater? What is greater than the forgiveness of sin? A failing of Wesley is that he held a diminished view of sin, and taking an inadequate view of sin, he took a low view of the blessing of forgiveness.

(3) It is instantaneous.

There is, Wesley said, a gradual preparation for sanctification and a growth in grace afterward—a concept which causes some problem because it means the perfection is imperfect—but the experience of sanctification itself is instantaneous; and one may have it "now, at this instant."[9] It is experienced in one (datable) moment, like a flash of lightning in its suddenness. With a great struggle one builds up to the point where he gives up reliance on every thing and places *absolute* trust in the Lord, then suddenly it comes—instantaneous sanctification. The "power" comes "in an instant" and "from that time they enjoy that inward and outward holiness, to which they were utter strangers before."[10]

(4) It is entire.

When one reaches this point (entire sanctification), he does not sin any more. He may make "mistakes" but the "mistakes" cannot properly be called sins. One now loves God perfectly, and when one's actions are prompted by nothing but love, they cannot be called sins.

> A mistake in judgment may possibly occasion a mistake in practice . . . Yet, where every word and action springs from love, such a mistake is not properly *a sin.*[11]

On this view, then, love reduces the absoluteness of the law. Wesley does not hesitate to use the word "perfect" to describe the "entirely sanctified."

> Christians are saved in this world from all sin, from all unrighteousness; . . . they are now in such a sense perfect as not to commit sin, and to be freed from evil thoughts and evil tempers.[12]

What diluted view of sin permits Wesley to deny that the "sanctified" do not commit it? He says flatly that "sin properly so called" is "a *voluntary* transgression of a *known* law."[13] In that case ignorance would be bliss? He then says plainly: "I believe a person filled with the love of God is still liable to . . . involuntary transgressions. Such transgressions you may call sins if you please. I do not. . . ."[14]

Wesley maintained that the entirely sanctified "are freed from evil thoughts, so that they cannot enter into them; no, not for a moment . . . there being no room for this in a soul which is full of God."[15] If this is true, it would be hard to imagine how a person could fall away. If evil thoughts cannot enter at all, even for a moment, how could one fall? Nevertheless, Wesley said that such sanctification was "capable of being lost."[16] He even said this "perfection" was "improvable."[17] But if it is "improvable," what does "perfection" mean?

He said further that the sanctified "have no fear or doubt, either as to their state in general or as to any particular action. The 'unction from the Holy One' [the Holy Spirit] teacheth them every hour what they shall do, and what they shall speak. Nor, therefore, have they any need to reason concerning it."[18] Weigh carefully the implications of that statement. What Wesley is saying is that the "perfect" man does not need to consult anything outside of himself—the standard of God—to determine whether he should do something. He has an inward speaking of the Spirit to guide his conduct. If a person were really to follow the implications of Wesley's statement, it might very well come to this: whatever I feel I want to do at the moment is what God is telling me to do. I am so full of God I cannot be tempted; so, whatever I am prompted to do, no matter what, must be God's prompting. Wesley's stated view here can easily lead to dispensing with an external standard (antinomianism), and in some people it has led to this.

How can a person know that he has reached this state of "Christian perfection"? Is a person not in danger of being deceived about this? Wesley's answer is: "Not at the time that he *feels* no sin. . . .So long as he feels nothing but love animating all his thoughts and words and actions, he is in no danger."[19] Again, Wesley asks: " 'But is there not *sin* in those that are *perfect*'?" and answers: "I believe not; but, be that as it may, they feel none, no temper but pure love, . . . And whether sin is *suspended* or *extinguished,* I will not dispute; it is enough that they feel nothing but love."[20] Do you remember the man of Luke 18? He "prayed": "God I thank thee, that I am not as the rest of men, extortioners, unjust, adulterers, or even as this publican. I fast twice in the week: I give tithes of all that I get" (Lk. 18:11,12). He was conscious of no sin in his life. Perhaps there is no sin more profound than thinking one has reached perfection.

Answer to Perfectionism

(1) Perfectionism mislocates entire sanctification.

Perfectionism is wrong in demanding to have "now," "at this instant" all the effects of our redemption. While redemption has been completed for us, its consummation in us awaits our glorification. Here and now, we live in "hope of the glory of God" (Rom. 5:2, 8:24,25) as we wait for the "redemption of our body" (Rom. 8:23, cf. Phil. 3:20,21) when we shall be raised from the dead and "this mortal" will put on "immortality" (I Cor. 15:53). Then we shall be made perfect in holiness (I John 3:2). Because of our hope, we now aspire to holiness and persevere in the struggle to be holy (I John 3:3). Sanctification is thus a part of the process of redemption which is perfected in the state of glory. Rather than insisting that we must have all the fruits of our redemption now, we rejoice in the "earnest" of our full inheritance (Eph. 1:14). Unwilling to wait, perfectionists, like impatient children, demand to get "in the first course" "all the feast prepared for them."[21]

(2) Perfectionism holds a superficial view of sin.

None of the greatest of God's servants rose above sin. Abraham lied about his wife to save himself (Gen. 12:13). He did this not once but twice (Gen. 20:2,13). Sarah lied to God, denying that she had laughed (Gen. 18:12-15). Aaron participated in making a golden calf (ex. 32:1-4) and pretended to be as surprised as anybody about what had happened (Ex. 32:24). The great Isaiah, awed by a sense of God's holiness, cried: "Woe is me! for I am undone; because I am a man of unclean lips, and I dwell in the midst of a people of unclean lips" (Is. 6:5; see also Lev. 16, I Kings 8:46, Ps. 14:3, Ecc. 7:20, Is. 53:6, 64:6).

In the face of this massive evidence of the magnitude and intensity of sin, Wesley can only say: But that was in the Old Testament; things are different in the New Testament.[22] But on this matter are things really different in the New Testament? Paul rebuked Peter because his fellow apostle was in the wrong, not in his doctrine, but in his failure to live up to his doctrine in regard to fellowship with the gentiles (Gal. 2:11-14). Jesus taught us to pray: "forgive us our debts" (Matt. 6:12). How long do we have need of that prayer? Paul said: "Christ Jesus came into the world to save sinners; of whom I am [not was] chief" (I Tim. 1:15). The apostle John said: "If we say we have no sin, we deceive ourselves, and the truth is not in us" (I John 1:8). The tense is present and the "we" certainly cannot be interpreted as referring to non-Christians. The Christian may not use the Biblical doctrine of sin to excuse sinning or to think lightly of it; he must realize that his warfare against sin has to be waged throughout his life in this world.

(3) Perfectionism has serious practical consequences.

(A) Perfectionism leads the sensitive, honest person to dispair (cf. Rom. 7:24). Have you ever heard anyone say: "I cannot become a Christian, because I could not live it"? Where did he get that idea?

(B) Not every person, however, is driven to hopelessness. The insensitive person becomes self-righteous (cf. Lk. 18:9-14). If he is perfect, others must be below him.

(C) Perfectionism inevitably creates two classes of Christians: the lower, nominal, carnal Christian; and the higher, complete, spiritual Christian. Dividing the body of Christ follows inescapably the dividing of our salvation (contrast I Cor. 12:12,13, Eph. 4:3-6).

(D) It always involves some kind of game playing or self-deception (I John 1:8). It has one living in a world of unreality—an unwholesome thing. Sins must become "mistakes," "omissions," "infirmities" instead of sins. "Christian perfection" must be defined as different from all other perfections, so that it becomes possible to be a "perfect Christian" without being a good man.[23] Religious good and moral good are separated.

(E) Closely related to the preceding point is the fact that perfectionism is always threatening to slide into antionomianism. One is strongly tempted to say: "Whatever I do is right because I am perfect." If I have absolute faith, perfect love, and am too full of God to sin, how can I ever conceive myself as being wrong?

(F) Perfectionism easily becomes, and often has become, quietism also. In quietism we become "quiet" before God and cease from our own efforts so God can work in us. We "let go and let God." Christ replaces us with himself and we turn over to him the living of the Christian life in us. The answer to quietism is Philippians 2:12,13: God's work in us is the reason for our work, not a substitute for it. Paul's exhortation is not: God is working; therefore, cease from effort. Rather, it is: work, for God is at work in you.

(G) Perfectionism is often responsible for breaking human relationships. Parents sometimes reject their children because they do not measure up to the parent's romantic expectations of them. Children, too, dismiss parents for the same reason. A husband or wife may discard his marriage because either the marriage or the partner has failed to meet his perfectionistic ideals. "I expected my marriage to be perfect," someone may say, "and now that I find it is not, all I can do is walk away from it." At times people abandon one congregation for another because they are trying to find a perfect congregation. Our relationships can be beautiful if we continue to work at them, but they can never be perfect. Sin constantly threatens and disrupts all relationships; we have constantly to restore and strengthen them.

62

A young woman came to her wedding expecting everything to be perfect. But things were going wrong.

> First the florist had dropped a basket of flowers, and even though he'd gathered them up and rearranged them, the basket on the right looked ragged compared with the one on the left. Then the bakery had used that hideous shade of blue. It was nothing like the color she'd picked out. The soloist had a cold, and to top it all off, she'd just stepped on the hem of her dress and pulled it loose at the waist. "It won't show a bit," her mother reassured her, but she knew it would. Her wedding day was ruined, and she had wanted everything to be so perfect. . . .

> Brenda's wedding was lovely. Everybody said so. It could have been for Brenda, too, if she had only forgotten her expectations and thankfully received the reality God provides.[24]

Her problem was perfectionism. The "unrealistic expectations" which ruined her wedding "will continue to operate in other areas of her life" and ruin them "unless she recognizes and deals with" them.[25]

Questions and Answers

1. What were the influences on John Wesley which led him to his conclusions about entire sanctification?

Wesley's views of spirituality and perfection were colored by the writings of early Eastern monks, by Platonism, and by the Moravians. From the Eastern monastic writings Wesley was convinced that ascetic discipline was the way to perfection. Wesley drew inspiration from the Platonic thought current in his day as well as from Plotinus himself and the monastic tradition of piety, which had itself been deeply influenced by Platonism—a view which disparages the "body" in the interest of the "soul." In Wesley's *Plain Account of Christian Perfection* the Platonic strain is evident in his expectation that "mistakes" are inevitable because "the corruptible body" "presses down the soul" (p. 28). The "desert fathers" whom Wesley so much admired, would no doubt have approved his refusal to allow the children to play in the school he founded. "If they play when they are boys," said Wesley, "they will play when they are men." This action shows an inadequate appreciation for the whole person. Wesley's association with the Moravians strengthened his tendency to emphasize inner feeling (the "witness of the Spirit") in religion and strongly encouraged his idea that man could rise above all sin.

2. What is the meaning of I John 3:9?

The passage gives no comfort to perfectionists—not, at least, to anyone who locates perfection in a "second work of grace"—for it says "whosoever," not "some." No "higher" experience is contemplated. If the passage teaches perfection, it teaches the perfection of every Christian. The key to understanding the passage is the tense of the participle "begotten" and the infinitive "sin" ("he cannot sin"). "Begotten" (*gegennemenos*) is perfect tense, which includes the two ideas of completed action and continuing result. It means, then: whoever has been begotten and continues to be affected by the fact. "Sin," in the phrase "cannot sin" is a present infinitive, which indicates continued action. John's statement is intended to correct the idea that it does not matter whether the Christian sins or not. The sense of the passage is: being begotten of God brings a change in a person's way of living. No one who has become a son or daughter of God can continue to sin—just as if being a child of God made no difference in behavior. Only such an understanding of the statement agrees with I John 1:8.

3. What did Jesus mean in Matthew 5:48: "be perfect?"

The rule of conduct cannot be popular misinterpretations of the law of God ("Ye have heard that it is said," v. 43, e.g.) or the example of the scribes and pharisees (v. 20) or of publicans and gentiles (46,47). The standard of Christian conduct is nothing less than the perfection of God himself. In no way is this standard to be lowered. The Christian is to aspire to reach it, strive for it, and measure himself by it. The problem comes when anyone says he has reached it.

4. Does I Corinthians 3:1 give us two kinds of Christians?

No, it does not. "Spiritual" and "carnal" here do not fix people in one of two changeless categories. Any Christian may have a "carnal" attitude on any matter at a particular time. This does not place him in the fixed category of "carnal," as opposed to another class of Christians who are always "spiritual." A person who is "carnal" this moment in his thinking or acting may the next moment correct himself and not be in the "carnal" category any longer. The same people in Corinth might be "carnal" at one time on one or more matters and "spiritual" at another time regarding the identical points. The categories are shifting, not fixed. They do not divide the church into two separate classes of Christians.

Questions to Guide Study

1. What is the meaning of justification? of sanctification?
2. Does the Biblical doctrine permit the separation of justification and sanctification, each received at different times? Cite specific passages in your answer.
3. What is Wesley's distinctive view of sanctification? How, according to Wesley, could a person reach it? How would one know he had reached it?
4. How does Wesley define sin? Evaluate his conception.
5. Do the Scriptures teach that the Christian will ever have entire sanctification? When?
6. Do Pentecostals themselves realize that their background is Wesleyan?
7. Do you believe that perfectionism may have serious practical consequences? Give some examples.

---

¹ Vinson Synan, *The Holiness-Pentecostal Movement in the United States* (Grand Rapids: Eerdmans, 1971), p. 8.

² Ibid., p. 13.

³ *The Letters of the Rev. John Wesley, A. M.,* ed. John Telford (London: The Epworth Press, 1931), VIII, 238 (letter of Sept. 1790), cited in Bruner, p. 323.

⁴ John Wesley, *A Plain Account of Christian Perfection* (1741; rev. ed. 1767), cited in Bruner, pp. 323 f.

⁵ Wesley, *Journal,* II (Sept. 13, 1739), cited in Bruner, p. 324.

⁶ Johannes Jungst, cited in Benjamin B. Warfield, *Perfectionism* (New York: Oxford University Press, 1931), II, 511, n. 121.

⁷ Wesley, *A Plain Account of Christian Perfection,* p. 47, cited in Bruner, p. 324.

⁸ Ibid., p. 53, cited in Bruner, p. 324.

⁹ Wesley, *Journal,* IV (Nov. 1, 1762: Letter to Thomas Maxfield, 536, cited in Bruner, p. 324.

¹⁰ Ibid., V (Aug. 27, 1768: Letter to Lawrence Coughlan), 284, cited in Bruner, p. 324 f.

¹¹ Wesley, *A Plain Account of Christian Perfection,* p. 43. cited in Bruner, p. 329.

¹² Wesley, "Christian Perfection" (a "sermon" published in 1741), p. 28, cited in *John Wesley,* ed. Albert C. Outler (New York: Oxford University Press, 1964), p. 270.

¹³ Wesley, "Thoughts on Christian Perfection," cited in Outler, p. 287. (The emphasis is added).

¹⁴ Ibid.

¹⁵ Wesley, *A Plain Account of Christian Perfection,* p. 23, cited in Bruner, p. 330.

¹⁶ Ibid., p. 106, cited in Bruner, p. 330.

¹⁷ Ibid.

¹⁸ Ibid., p. 23, cited in Bruner, p. 330.

¹⁹ Ibid., p. 57, cited in Bruner, p. 325, n. 10. (The emphasis is added).

²⁰ Wesley, *Letters,* IV (To Mrs. Maitland, May 12, 1763), 213, cited in Bruner, p. 328. (The emphasis is Wesley's).

²¹ Warfield, II, 537.

²² Wesley, "Christian Perfection," 10-13, cited in Outler, pp. 261-263.

²³ Warfield, II, 528 and n. 159.

²⁴ Billie Silvey, "Expectations," *Twentieth Century Christian* (September 1979), 17-18.

²⁵ Ibid., p. 18.

CHAPTER VIII

The Meaning and Development of Pentecostalism

Pentecostalism grew out of eighteenth century Methodism. John Wesley laid the foundation for Pentecostalism when he divided salvation into two parts (justification and sanctification) with no intrinsic connection between them and taught people to set their hearts on a higher experience after justification. He also contributed the doctrine of perfectionism and the idea that experience is the means of the assurance of salvation. It has its roots also in American frontier revivalism of the early nineteenth century and the holiness crusade of the latter half of the nineteenth century. The Pentecostal Synan says: "Basically, the pentecostal movement is an heir of the frontier, enthusiastic type of religion that has been indigenous to the American religious experience. . . . It also is an attempt to perpetuate the doctrine of perfectionism which dominated Protestantism during the nineteenth century, as well as the tradition of revivalism that loomed so large in the last century and the early part of the twentieth century."[1] The development of Pentecostalism is summarized briefly in the following family tree:

> Wesleyanism (eighteenth century)
> Revivalism (early nineteenth century)
> The Holiness Movement (latter nineteenth century)
> Pentecostalism (1901)
> Neo-Pentecostalism (1950's)

Revivalism

Revivalism is Wesleyanism preached in a distinctive way on the American frontier. A foremost representative of revivalistic preaching is Charles G. Finney (1792-1876), who second to Wesley exerted the greatest influence on Pentecostalism. Finney added no significant new doctrine; his contribution was a greater degree of emotionalism as the conscious way of bringing people to "spiritual crisis." Finney believed that preaching should excite people and "sweep" them into religious experience. Revivalism means revival by excitement. Finney said:

> God has found it necessary to take advantage of the excitability there is in mankind to produce powerful excitements among them before he can lead them to obey. Men are so sluggish, there are so many things to lead their

minds off from religion and to oppose the influence of the gospel that it is necessary to raise an excitement among them till the tide rises so high as to sweep away the opposing obstacles.[2]

Finney obviously did not place his emphasis on content and persuading people of the truth of Christianity. In his understanding the preacher's ability to excite people becomes the power of God to salvation.

There are several problems inherent in Finney's approach. In a state of excitement people can be "swept" into anything. Further, religious conversion produced by excitement rather than the word of God only leads people into feverish activity, not to stable Christian development. Another problem with revival by excitement is that when the initial enthusiasm wanes, without more and greater excitements, the person is left in a state of despair.

Revivalist preaching raised people to such a fever pitch emotionally that they manifested strange motor phenomena. Such manifestations were generally called "godly hysteria"; some called them "Methodist fits." It was believed that such hysteria came as a result of conviction brought by the Spirit of God. Sometimes people would get the "jerks" and shake violently in every part of their body. At times they would swoon or fall into trances and lie for hours. These were called the "slain of the Lord" or the "smitten of the Lord." At other times the erratic behavior would take the form of the "holy laugh" (whole congregations would laugh uncontrollably for long periods), convulsions, shouting, screaming, wild dancing (called the "holy dance"), jumping like frogs, "treeing the devil." When "treeing the devil," men and women would get down on all fours at the foot of a tree, growl and bark like dogs. Another motor response was a rapid, emotion laden, unintelligible speaking. This was called "speaking in tongues" and was said to be identical with what happened in the second chapter of Acts. Incomprehensibly, all of these strange actions were applauded and encouraged on the ground that they had spiritual value.

Another outcome of the ferment produced by the revivalism of the early nineteenth century was Mormonism. It is "generally known that Mormonism had its beginning in this region [of New York], but it is not so generally understood, I think that Mormonism was literally born and bred in the unhealthy revival atmosphere" of the period.[3] The Mormons "experienced much the same motor phenomena that characterized the early Methodists and later pentecostals. Shouting, jerks, and dancing were common in their services, and Brigham Young not only spoke in unknown tongues, but interpreted his own messages to his hearers. Mormon choirs were even known to sing in unknown tongues."[4]

The Holiness Movement

Pentecostalism came most directly from the holiness revival of the second half of the nineteenth century. This revival saw a number of movements arise, including the "higher life" movement and the "victorious life" movement, all with the purpose of restoring Wesley's emphasis on entire sanctification. The most influential book in the literature of the holiness movement was W. E. Boardman's *The Higher Christian Life,* published in 1859. Boardman maintained that by "full trust" we receive "full salvation" in a "second conversion," a "deeper work of grace." The holiness movement identified the "second conversion" with the "baptism in the Holy Spirit," and so popularized the expression which is characteristic of Pentecostalism.

Toward the end of the century more than a score of separate holiness denominations were formed out of the movement. The largest of these was the Nazarene Church—a holiness, not pentecostal, church. It, rather than the United Methodist Church, represents the original Wesleyan teaching. The primary concerns of the holiness movement can perhaps best be summed up from the statement on "Entire Sanctification" in the *Nazarene Manual* (1972):

> We believe that entire sanctification is the act of God, subsequent to regeneration, by which believers are made free from original sin, or depravity, and brought into a state of entire devotement to God, and the holy obedience of love made perfect.
>
> It is wrought by the baptism with the Holy Spirit, and comprehends in one experience the cleansing of the heart from sin and the abiding indwelling presence of the Holy Spirit, empowering the believer for life and service.
>
> Entire sanctification is provided by the blood of Jesus, is wrought instantaneously by faith, preceded by entire consecration; and to this work and state of grace the Holy Spirit bears witness.
>
> This experience is also known by various terms representing its different phases, such as "Christian perfection," "perfect love," "heart purity," "the baptism with the Holy Spirit," "the fullness of the blessing," and "Christian holiness."

The Wesleyan emphases are clear: sanctification is "entire," "subsequent," "is wrought instantaneously," and is obviously higher since it brings "entire devotement to God," and grants power for "life and service" (which one did not have before though he was in Christ?); moreover, in thorough Wesleyan fashion, certainty of this "state of grace" is brought by the witness of the

Spirit. Note that the "faith" by which sanctification is received is not the simple faith in the gospel exercised at conversion, but is faith that has become absolute, a faith that involves "entire consecration." Observe also the important point that in holiness thought "entire sanctification" and "baptism with the Holy Spirit" are identical.

Summary of the Religious Atmosphere Which Gave Rise to Pentecostalism

Two characteristics are held in common by the religious developments we have been considering: experientialism and perfectionism. Experientialism means simply that religion is centered in experience and feeling. The great drama that takes place in the heart of the believer is the focal point in experiential religion. What is used to determine doctrine or the content of religion is experience—that is, the experientialist will say: "I have had this marvelous experience which has transformed my life and brought me peace; it must be from God." The Bible is then read in the light of the experience. How does one know he is saved? The experientialist answers: "By the dramatic experience of having Christ come into your heart and change you." What the experientalist preacher offers is an inner experience that is dramatic and thrilling. "Are you satisfied with your religion?" he asks. "Let me tell you some "steps," and "keys," and "secrets" that you may use to find a satisfying experience. What is being offered is "the victorious Christian life," "the exciting discovery of the Spirit-filled life," "the higher Christian life." That is experientialism.

The second characteristic of these religious traditions is perfectionism, which, as we have seen, means that one reaches the point in his life when his faith becomes absolute and his commitment to the Lord is entire. Or, to speak as the perfectionists do, "You lay it all on the altar before the Lord." Then you have reached the point where you do not sin any more though you may make "mistakes." According to this view, when you become a Christian, you are an incomplete Christian. Later you decide to lay it all on the altar and you become a complete Christian. And great things begin to happen in your life when you reach this point, whereas everything is rather "blah" before you reach that critical point.

Such experiential and perfectionistic religion was widespread toward the close of the nineteenth century. But a feeling of elation is hard to maintain, often varies, and can be misleading; and looking to the change in one's life as evidence of salvation is hardly satisfying. In this atmosphere there were people who pushed beyond Wesley's "inner witness" to find an experience that would verify beyond question that they had found the "higher" or

69

"victorious Christian life." The people who pushed further in search of evidence more empirical than Wesley's "crisis experience" deeply felt in the heart found it in the evidence of "tongues." The addition of this evidence to the body of experiential and perfectionistic material inherited from Wesley marks the birth of Pentecostalism. Thus the passion for "more" which brought Pentecostalism into existence at the first is the same passion which leads people into it today.

The Meaning of Pentecostalism

Pentecostalism made its first definite appearance on January 1, 1901, at Charles Fox Parham's Bethel Bible School, where he had gathered a few months earlier about forty holiness students. Parham added to existing holiness belief the idea that "speaking in tongues" is *the evidence* of "full" salvation. The addition of tongues occasioned a slight alteration in accepted holiness teaching: the "baptism in the Holy Spirit" was not "entire sanctification"; it was rather a third experience. When Agnes N. Ozman, a young woman at Parham's school, had the ecstatic experience of "speaking in tongues," it meant the introduction of a new element into religious thought. The new factor was the expectation that tongues would be given as proof of the Spirit's reception. Both tongues and Spirit baptism had been claimed before, but not in Parham's new combination. It is the joining of these two things which divides Pentecostalism from the holiness movement and makes Pentecostalism what it is. The new religion began to flourish in the 1906 "Los Angeles revival" under the influence of W. J. Seymour, one of Parham's students in the school he opened in Houston, Texas in 1905.

The distinctive and fundamental element in Pentecostal belief finds expression in the following statement of faith:

> We believe . . . that the full gospel includes holiness of heart and life, healing for the body, and the baptism in the Holy Spirit with the initial evidence of speaking in other tongues as the Spirit gives utterance.[5]

The crucial phrase in the statement is "full gospel." The Pentecostal conviction is that others preach a "simple gospel" of "mere" forgiveness grounded on the redemptive action of Christ (I Cor. 15:1-5). There is a "full gospel" beyond this gospel. The Pentecostal "full gospel" has three elements:

(1) "holiness of heart and life." Every Christian believes in "holiness of heart and life" as a fruit of the gospel. But the Pentecostal understands the words in the Wesleyan sense of entire sanctification as a second blessing. The Pentecostal feels that he is preaching the gospel when he testifies to or shares his extraordinary

70

religious experience and triumphs which show the marvelous change that has taken place in his life. His own experiences, rather than Christ's, become the "full gospel." The gospel becomes the gospel of his changed life.

(2) "healing for the body." Physical healing is believed to be not only a promise for the person with "full faith," but is held to be a part of the gospel—the "full gospel." When the Pentecostal preaches "healing for the body" and exhorts people to claim this blessing, in his view, he is preaching the gospel.

(3) "baptism in the Holy Spirit with the initial evidence of . . . tongues." Before Pentecostalism tongue-speaking was regarded as only one among many evidences that one had "come under the power of God." Pentecostalism gives it a new significance. It is not the "holy laugh" or "swooning" or "treeing the devil" which proves the reception of the Spirit, but tongue-speaking is the only initial evidence. The word "initial" is important in Pentecostal understanding. "Speaking in tongues" is believed to be the first proof given of the Spirit's full coming. It is the only initial evidence there is. A person may afterwards receive other evidences in the form of various gifts.

Neo-Pentecostalism

In 1953 a group called the "Full Gospel Business Men's Fellowship, International" was formed. As "full gospel" in the name suggests, the association is Pentecostal. The Full Gospel Business Men's Fellowship had meetings in pleasant hotel accommodations, with a number of people, both Pentecostal and non-Pentecostal, invited to attend. They would have breakfast together and afterwards a meeting that usually lasted for a considerable time. People who had had the "Pentecostal experience" would give their testimony. A typical testimony would run like this: "I was in dire straits, really in desperate trouble. My marriage was on the rocks. I was in financial difficulty. I was in poor health. I was at my wit's end. I did not know where I could turn next. My heart was hungry. Then I had this remarkable experience. It was wonderful! And my life has never been the same since. This satisfying, thrilling experience brought strength into my life. Everything is different now. This transforming experience filled me with power to testify of my faith in Jesus. It brought peace to my heart and made me love God. My business is prospering. I don't feel just half alive anymore. I'm on fire for the Lord!"

There were non-Pentecostals listening who said: "You know, I need something, too. I am about as desperate. I am spiritually starved. I see very little evidence of power in my life. And I am inept in my efforts to share my faith in Christ. I need what these people have received. I wish I could have a glowing experience like

71

theirs to tell." In this way Pentecostalism began to spread among people outside the Pentecostal denominations. The people from other groups who have experienced the "Pentecostal phenomenon" are called Neo-Pentecostals or charismatics. The Neo-Pentecostal might be a Presbyterian, an Episcopalian, a Methodist, a Baptist, a Catholic (since 1967), or any other. The Neo-Pentecostal is anyone in any religious group who has had what he calls the "baptism in the Holy Spirit" (the Catholic speaks of the "actualization of the Spirit") with the evidence of "speaking in tongues." This is his great and primary experience. He adjusts the other doctrines around this as best he can. The traditional Pentecostal is in a group identifiable as Pentecostal, such as the Assemblies of God or the Church of God. The Neo-Pentecostal is in any group at all and may be a minister, a physician, a professor, a prominent and successful businessman, or any other kind of professional person.

It would be interesting, wouldn't it, to know how a traditional or an old line Pentecostal reacts to the new Pentecostals. Ray Hughes, a traditional Pentecostal, has written an article in which he tells us. Ray Hughes is general overseer of the Church of God (Cleveland, Tennessee). He tells us that there is concern among the older Pentecostals about the new Pentecostals. Hughes finds the Neo-Pentecostals too experience-oriented.[6] The classic Pentecostal is too experiential. Pentecostalism originated by running past the holiness movement in its experientialism. But the new Pentecostal has gone beyond the old Pentecostal. The traditional Pentecostals at least confess faith in infallible Scripture and hold that there are some other doctrines which must be believed—doctrines such as the deity of Christ, his bodily resurrection, the general resurrection, and judgment. The new Pentecostal is different. He holds that the one indispensable thing is that one have the "experience of God." Nothing one may believe beyond this is absolutely essential. Hughes rightly says: "The Word of God is the means by which experience is authenticated."[7] Every Pentecostal should understand that and act on it. Every non-Pentecostal should understand that and act on it.

Hughes is uneasy over the fact that "there is a claim to the Pentecostal experience among the liberal movements."[8] A classic Pentecostal once said about a new Pentecostal, "This man is so liberal he does not even believe in the resurrection of Christ." "I wonder," he said, "why God has given him all this power. I cannot understand it." This ought to cause a person real concern as he thinks about what is going on—what this experience really is.

Another thing that disturbs the old Pentecostal is that Catholics lay claim to the "Pentecostal experience." And this makes them better Catholics. "According to a number of Catholic writers, Catholic Pentecostals tend to go back and begin using avenues of contact with God that they had abandoned—the rosary, the Real Presence, devotion to Mary."[9] The Real Presence means that in the celebration of the Mass the bread is turned into the actual body of Christ, the wine into the actual blood of Christ, and Christ is re-sacrificed. Some Catholics report that the Spirit falls upon them with great power "in prayer to the Blessed Virgin."[10] Now that creates grave problems for anyone who believes that Jesus Christ is the only mediator between God and man. If Christ is the only Mediator, how could the Spirit come during devotion to the "Blessed Virgin," the "Mother of God"? If the Spirit is the Spirit of truth, can he tolerate just anything that is put forward in his name? Does the Spirit indeed recognize any other Mediator than Christ? If not, that raises the question, has the Catholic received the Spirit? If you answer no, he has not received the Spirit, then what about the Pentecostal himself? The Catholic does the same things as the Pentecostal. He has the same outward manifestations. This raises problems for the old Pentecostal and the new Pentecostal as well.

Hughes finds distressing the fact that the charismatics have a "tendency to place revelations on a level with the Word or even above it." He then says that "it must always be pointed out that true revelations are not contrary to the Word, nor do they supplant the Word."[11] But what we should ask is this, are there revelations today? And if a person believes there are revelations today, how could he help but place them "on a level" with the word or "even above it"? If I believe a revelation is being given to me directly from God, how could I possibly avoid putting it on a par with Scripture? Or above it? In Pentecostalism as well as in Neo-Pentecostalism the sufficiency of the word is denied. Anybody who relies at all on present revelations does not believe in the sufficiency of the word.

A final statement from Hughes deserves careful consideration: "The Word of God sets forth not an experience-oriented Pentecost but a Word-centered Pentecost. Scripture is not verified by experience; rather, experience is tested by Scripture."[12] Indeed that is true, but it is rather puzzling coming from a Pentecostal. On Pentecost the apostle Peter did not begin by saying: "Let me tell you about an experience I just had that thrilled me throughout my being. I want to tell you how you, too, can have it." He began by saying: "Ye men of Israel, hear these words: Jesus of Nazareth. . . ." (Acts 2:22).

Questions and Answers

1. What is the meaning of the word "charismatic"?

Charismatic is from the Greek word *charisma,* which means literally "a thing of grace." *Charisma* is derived from *charis,* "grace." *Charisma* is used in Scripture of a gracious gift of God. It is translated "free gift" in Roman 6:23 and simply "gift" in I Corinthians 7:7. In I Corinthians 12:4 Paul uses the word in an effort to correct the Corinthians' view that gifts of the Spirit were rewards for human merit.

Far removed from the New Testament usage is the common statement that someone has "charisma"—the ability to excite people as if by magic.

Neo-Pentecostals use "charismatic" to mean the extraordinary gifts of the Spirit. Some Neo-Pentecostals prefer this word in an effort to avoid the associations of frenzy connected with the word "Pentecostal."

2. Are the people who teach this second work of grace sincere? If so, should we condemn them?

Yes, I assume they are sincere, because it is beyond my province to do otherwise. We may insist strongly that an idea is wrong without questioning a person's sincerity. Heresy taught by an honest man is still heresy. In fact, it may be all the more dangerous.

The way we answer this question reflects our basic conception of Christianity. If Christianity is only a way of meeting our functional needs, then the only question we need to ask is whether a belief meets someone's felt needs or not. Does it make him feel well, bring integration to his personality, give him a sense of value? If so, for him it is true, even though for me it may not be true.

But if Christianity is a revelation of truth from God, then it is true objectively, and the law of antithesis applies—that is, whatever is contrary to this revealed truth is false.

II Thessalonians 2:9-12 teaches that a person may believe the most outrageous lie as a judgment from God if he refuses to believe the truth. Many who stand and give their testimonies may really no longer be able to tell what is objectively true or false.

Questions to Guide Study

1. What is the genealogy of Pentecostalism?
2. What does Pentecostalism mean by the "full gospel"? Evaluate its view of the gospel.

3. Evaluate Finney's view of preaching. Does such preaching really bring a person to Christ?
4. What did Pentecostalism derive from Wesleyanism? from revivalism? the holiness movement?
5. Does Pentecostalism differ from the holiness movement in its fundamental religious beliefs? How is it different?
6. What is experientialism?
7. How does Neo-Pentecostalism differ from traditional Pentecostalism?

---

[1] Synan, p. 223.
[2] Cited in Bruner, p. 41.
[3] F. M. Davenport, cited in Warfield, II, 228.
[4] Synan, p. 25f.
[5] "The Constitution of the Pentecostal Fellowship of North America," in F. E. Mayer, *The Religious Bodies of America,* p. 319, cited in Bruner, p. 20, n. 2.
[6] Ray H. Hughes, "A Traditional Pentecostal Looks at the New Pentecostals," *Christianity Today,* XVIII (June 1974), 1036-1040.
[7] Ibid., p. 1037.
[8] Ibid., p. 1036.
[9] Ibid., p. 1040.
[10] Ibid.
[11] Ibid.
[12] Ibid., p. 1037.

CHAPTER IX

Evaluation of Pentecostalism: Is It Biblical?

Pentecostalism's experiential nature and perfectionistic base, as well as its separation of justification and sanctification, have been treated already in the course of developing its origin and meaning. Its claim to tongue speaking and miracles will be discussed in separate chapters. The present study will examine several other distinguishing features of Pentecostalism and evaluate them in the light of Scripture.

Pentecostalism Undervalues the Gospel

The foundation of the whole Pentecostal system is the conviction that one does not become a complete Christian at conversion. Pentecostalism therefore feels the need for a "full gospel"—"good news" beyond the "simple gospel" of Christ's death for our sins—which is able to bring fulness. Every convert to Pentecostalism first experiences a deep "hunger of heart" for more than "mere" forgiveness of sins received in Christ. Note the idea of "more" in the following typical Pentecostal statements, the first by the Swedish Pentecostal Lewi Pethrus:

> I not only understand that there *was* more for me, but felt there *must* be more for *me,* or otherwise my Christian life would be a failure. My Christian life was not satisfying to God nor to myself. Of this I was fully convinced . . . there was more to be had.[1]

Similarly Thomas Barratt, who received his experience in 1906 and who founded the Pentecostal movement in Norway, says:

> When praying I constantly felt the need of a *still greater blessing over my own soul!* . . . I knew there must be a *still deeper work and a constant victory.*[2]

The Neo-Pentecostal John Osteen says:

> I stand as one of the group of pastors who are desperately concerned and deeply disturbed over the lack of power . . . there has been a growing concern in my heart, for I knew that something ought to be there which was not

76

there. . . . I read in the Bible about the early church and its supernatural power and I so longed for such as that.[3]

The Pentecostal longs to move beyond forgiveness or "salvation theology" (or even "hang-up" as it is sometimes called) to an experience of power. Whenever anyone diminishes the concept of sin, in the same act he reduces the blessing of forgiveness and undercuts the value of Christ's work in securing forgiveness—the work which is the living center of Christianity. There can be no greater error.

A few years ago I had a discussion with a young man who was the leader of the "Jesus movement" (a charismatic group) in Nashville. As we talked, I asked him: "Why do you think I need the miraculous gifts and stirring spiritual experiences which you told me you have?"

"Ah," he answered, "you would have a heart-knowledge of God, not just a head-knowledge, and you would feel so much more intimate with God."

"Do you know what I am sure I have in Christ?" I asked him. "Perhaps I do not," he said.

We considered the meaning of Paul's statement in Galatians 2:20: "that life which I now live in the flesh I live in faith, the faith which is in the Son of God, who loved me, and gave himself up for me." "To Paul," I told him, "this was Christ's supreme action, and this is what Christ did for me. He did not heal my blindness or lameness as he did for some people during his ministry. He did something greater: he 'loved me and gave himself up for me.' What can he do for me now greater than that?"

"Well," he said, "maybe you do have something after all."

The Christian should stand in awe before what Christ has done already rather than set his heart on an experience which he thinks Christ may give him today. Doing the latter would fail to appreciate the magnitude of the fact that Christ gave himself for us. It would shift the whole center of gravity in the New Testament.

Pentecostalism Mislocates Fulness

Pentecostalism's "full gospel" and its felt need for "more"—more than one receives initially in Christ—means that only part-life is found in Christ. To become complete the person who is already in Christ needs an experience of the Spirit beyond his initial experience of being in Christ. An error very similar to this was being taught in Colossae. This Colossian heresy taught Christians how to be complete by meeting conditions beyond being in Christ. Included in the steps and secrets to the full life were (1) keeping certain rituals (Col. 2:16,17), (2) emptying oneself (practicing a false humility or self-abasement) so one could become full (2:18), (3) cultivating ecstatic visions in which one supposedly experienced God and from which one derived a sense of elation (2:18b), and (4) practicing extreme asceticism ("severity to the body," 2:20-23. Fasting is a recognized way of achieving ecstasy).

Paul's answer is that fulness is received in Christ, not by meeting conditions beyond being in Christ. "For in him dwelleth all the fulness of the Godhead bodily, and in him ye are made full" (Col. 2:9,10). God gives fulness in Christ at baptism (2:12) in which he makes alive (not half alive) and forgives all trespasses (2:13) because of Christ's accomplishment for us (2:14,15). In verses 9 and 10 there is a play on the word "fulness" (*pleroma* = "fulness," or "completeness"). All the completeness (*pleroma*) of Deity resides permanently in Christ and in him (emphatic) Christians are complete (*pepleromenoi*). The verb is perfect tense. It means therefore not "you are being made complete" but "you have been made complete" (perfected action) "and so you are now complete" (present consequence). The completeness refers to our objective standing before God, not to our subjective condition or commitment, which is complete only at our glorification. In the realization of his completeness before God, the Christian does not consider his life to be poverty-stricken. Instead of hungering for "more," he goes forth to serve God with assurance and joy and thanksgiving (Col. 3:1-17).

Parallel to Colossians 2:10 is Paul's statement in Ephesians 1:3: "Blessed be the God and Father of our Lord Jesus Christ, who hath blessed us with every spiritual blessing in the heavenly places in Christ." It is not the case that God has blessed us with a few or several blessings in Christ and we are to cultivate a longing for more and press on until we get "God's best" for us. Rather, he has blessed us with "every spiritual blessing" in Christ. Paul explains what is included in "every spiritual blessing" in verses 4-14: (1) We are chosen in Christ (v. 4), and (2) redeemed in Christ (v. 7). (3) We have a knowledge of "the mystery of his will" revealed in Christ (v. 9). (4) In him we are God's "heritage" or possession (v. 11) and (5) in Christ we have received the Spirit as "the earnest of our inheritance" (13,14). This impressive array of blessings leaves only one benefit to which the Christian looks forward—the consummation of his salvation in the state of glory. There is no other "second blessing" than this.

Pentecostalism Misconceives the Work of the Spirit

A corollary of Pentecostalism's misconceiving and undervaluing the work of Christ is its misconception of the work of the Spirit. When the Spirit came, Jesus taught, he would bring to remembrance what Christ had said (John 14:26); he would testify of Christ (John 15:26) and bring men to faith in Christ (John

16:8-11)—in short, he would glorify Christ, as in the summary of Jesus (John 16:14). And this means more than putting "Praise the Lord" and "Thank you, Jesus" at the end of a testimony to some marvelous personal experience.

Pentecostal teaching is a reverse of Biblical doctrine. A traditional Pentecostal, John Lake, says:

> The outpouring of the Holy Ghost is the greatest event in Christian history—greater than the crucifixion, of greater import than the resurrection, greater than the ascension, greater than the glorification. It was the end and finality which the crucifixion, resurrection and glorification sought to accomplish.[4]

This is to rewrite the New Testament. It has Christ pointing beyond himself to the work of the Spirit, whereas the New Testament has the Spirit pointing away from himself to Christ. Pentecostalism has relocated and therefore mislocated the focal point in Christianity.

Under the heading "My Personal Experience" Lake continues:

> I knelt under a tree when about sixteen years of age in repentance and prayer, and God came into my soul. I was saved from my sins, and from that day I knew Jesus Christ as a living Saviour. There never was a single moment of question about the reality of his coming into my life as a Savior.[5]

It is important to note that he had no doubt that Christ had come into his life as Savior. But that was not the end of his quest. He says that he was some time afterwards given the experience of sanctification and the "ministry of healing," and "ministered for ten years in the power of God."

> But at the end of that ten years I believe I was the hungriest man for God that ever lived.[6]

He has said Christ was in his life; he was sure of that, but he was still "the hungriest man for God that ever lived." Does it seem strange to you that a man could have Christ in his life and yet be "the hungriest man for God" in the world?

> There was such a hunger for God that as I left my offices in Chicago and walked down the street, my soul would break out and I would cry, "Oh, God!" I have had people stop and look at me and wonder.

The idea here is desperately wrong. Contrast the statement of Jesus:

> I am the bread of life: he that cometh to me shall not

hunger, and he that believeth on me shall never thirst
(John 6:35).

How could a person who has Christ be the hungriest man for God
in the world? Did he not meet God in Christ? Did he not draw near
enough to God in Christ? If a person cannot find God in Christ,
can he find him anywhere? The Christian realizes that without
Christ he was starving for want of communion with God, but in
Christ he has come to know God and has peace with God. His
attitude is one of thanksgiving for the relationship he has with God
in Christ, not despair because he is without God. If anyone has a
hunger that Christ cannot satisfy, there is something wrong with
the hunger. Or it may be that such a person never really knew
Christ.

What Lake says he had in Christ was "nice as far as it went," but
it was not "answering the cry" of his heart. The satisfaction for his
hunger which he had not found in Christ he says he finally found in
the "baptism in the Holy Ghost."

> I spoke in tongues by the power of God, and God flowed
> through me with a new force. Healings were of a more
> powerful order. Oh, God lived in me; God manifested in
> me; God spoke through me. My spirit was deified. . . .[8]

Lake says he received such great power that if people came near
him, they would feel that power and be overcome by it; if he only
pointed his finger at them, they might fall down as if they were
dead.

> God came over my life in such power, in such streams of
> liquid glory and power that it flowed consciously off my
> hands like streams of electricity. I could point my finger at
> a man, and that stream would strike him. When a man
> interrupted the meeting, I pointed my finger at him and
> said, "Sit down!" He fell as if struck and lay for three
> hours. When he became normal, they asked him what had
> happened, and he said, "Something struck me that went
> straight through me. I thought I was shot."[9]

Pentecostalism obviously directs the attention of men beyond
Christ to the power of the Spirit and powerful manifestations of the
Spirit as evidence of his presence. Because Pentecostalism is wrong
about the work of the Holy Spirit—to fix attention on Christ—it is
wrong also about the evidence of the Spirit. It has developed what
might be called "charisma-mania," a preoccupation with
extraordinary gifts of the Spirit. This is the Corinthian heresy.

Pentecostalism Is Wrong About the Conditions for Receiving the Spirit

Lake is giving typical Pentecostal conditions when he says: "The requirement is a surrendered heart, a surrendered mind, a surrendered life."[10] He is speaking of a total yielding that comes after conversion. When he became convinced of the supreme value of the experience, he determined that he was "going to possess it" and "went into fasting and prayer and waiting on God for nine months."[11] Relating how the Pentecostal experience was received in Africa, Donald Gee wrote:

> Oh, how they cried and groaned and groveled in the dust, as they wrestled their way to victory. The noise of this great visitation was heard in a village a mile and a half away.[12]

Pentecostalism's long list of conditions includes, after conversion, desiring the Spirit more than anything else in the world, absolute faith, obedience, and surrender, cleansing the heart of all sin, faith in the Spirit's coming, and prayer, often agonizing, for the Spirit. In spite of all these conditions the Spirit is said to be received without being deserved, as a gift.

According to the New Testament the Spirit is a gift graciously given at conversion, not received by agonizing human effort as a subsequent experience. The Spirit is received in the beginning (Gal. 3:3) by "the hearing of faith" (Gal. 3:2). The means of receiving the Spirit is simple faith in Christ, not faith that has become absolute (John 7:37-39). The Spirit is given when one becomes a Christian, at the point of baptism (Acts 2:38, I Cor. 12:13). When is one better prepared to receive the Spirit than when God has washed away his sins (Acts 22:16)?

Pentecostalism Misunderstands the Meaning of New Testament Baptism

Pentecostalism has divided the New Testament's one baptism into two. The "first" is spoken of as only baptism in water. And it is a symbol without vital spiritual content. But there is a "second" baptism that really has spiritual value—the "baptism of the Spirit." In the "first" baptism in mere water the believer makes a profession of his faith and engages to be obedient to God. In the "second," higher baptism God acts to give the Spirit. Because the Pentecostal misunderstands the meaning of the New Testament baptism, he seeks a baptism that does have meaning.

"Thus in water baptism," says a Pentecostal statement, "which is an action from our side, *we* seal God's trustworthiness, and in the Spirit-baptism, which is an action from God's side, *he* places

81

the seal upon our sincerity . . . ."[13]

> The difference between the two baptisms is that commitment receives a more symbolic interpretation in water-baptism while in Spirit-baptism the consecration is felt experientially. In water-baptism *we* bear witness that we firmly trust God's promises of grace. In Spirit-baptism, however, *God* confesses himself openly to *us* . . . .[14]

"Water baptism" is seen only as an action which we do—a conception which misunderstands baptism from the start. It is not understood (as the New Testament understands it) as the place where God acts to bestow all his rich blessings on us: the forgiveness of sins and the gift of the Holy Spirit (Acts 2:38), justification and sanctification (I Cor. 6:11), new birth (John 3:5), renewal (Titus 3:5), death to sin and power for life (Rom. 6-8). Only in the "Spirit baptism" is God seen as acting. Pentecostalism has separated (as did the thought world from which it sprang) the water and the Spirit and made two baptisms. One means very little, and the other means everything. But in Ephesians 4:5 Paul states there is "one baptism." Since in baptism we receive the fulness of spiritual blessings, there can be no reason for a second baptism. The New Testament's one baptism is a rock on which Pentecostalism breaks apart.

In the context of Ephesians 4:5 Paul appeals to Christians "to keep the unity of the Spirit in the bond of peace" (v. 3). Christians are not taught to create a unity; they are told to preserve the unity which the gospel creates. Now, what is the basis of this unity? "There is one body, and one Spirit, even as also ye were called in one hope of your calling; one Lord, one faith, one baptism, one God and Father of all, who is over all, and through all, and in all" (4-6). Paul goes on to say there are differences. "But unto each one of us was the grace given according to the measure of the gift of Christ" (v. 7), and he names the different gifts: "he gave some to be apostles; and some, prophets; and some evangelists; and some, pastors and teachers" for the good of the whole church (v. 11).

We do differ in this respect: we have different functions because we have different gifts. But in regard to the fundamentals of Christianity we do not differ, and therein is our unity. We should strive to maintain our unity because there is only "one body" of Christians (not two consisting of lower and higher Christians), "one Spirit," whom all Christians received equally upon entering the "one body," "one hope" of glorification which the call by the gospel implanted in all alike. There is "one Lord," Jesus Christ in whom we believe and "one faith" directed to the "one Lord," the object of the Christian's faith. There is "one baptism" in which we all confessed the "one faith" and received the "one Spirit," and there is "one God," whom we all worship.

82

Try reading the passage this way: " 'Keep the unity of the Spirit in the bond of peace,' and the basis of unity is this: 'there is one body, and one Spirit,' even as your calling leads you to hope for one and the same thing, 'one Lord, one faith,' two baptisms, 'one God.' All of you have received the first baptism, and the really dedicated have received a second. Therefore, there is unity; now, you preserve it." That is no basis for unity; it introduces two classes of Christians, with some on one level and others on a higher level. The concept of two baptisms necessarily introduces disunity. How can Pentecostalism ever justify its two baptisms in the face of Ephesians 4:5?

The following statement from a careful student of Pentecostalism deserves serious consideration:

> The rediscovery of the meaning of New Testament baptism is of the highest importance if aberrations offering "more" are to be resisted and if the church is to be itself. For Pentecostalism is an illustration of the fact that where the biblical one-baptism is emptied of its content other substitutes and supplements—other baptisms—rush in to fill the vacuum. Where the one-baptism is not the sufficient seal of certainty, then other certainties, other evidences *must* be found, for the certainty of salvation is a major human concern.[15]

Pentecostalism Improperly Uses Scripture

Pentecostalism, both old and new, undervalues and misuses the word of God. It commonly places experience over the word and, neglecting the sufficiency of Scripture, is always threatening to exalt present revelations to a level with or even above holy Scripture. It does not encourage a careful study of Scripture to find the meaning of Scripture. While Neo-Pentecostalism commonly uses Scripture as a channel for religious experience, the traditional Pentecostal again and again assigns meanings to passages without regard to their historical context or the flow of thought in the larger movement of ideas. Approaching the Bible to discover its own meaning rather than to reinforce our own ideas and support our experiences is fundamental. It is the only way to treat the Bible seriously, and without such an approach there is no means of validating any religious belief or correcting ourselves in any error. This is true for the Pentecostal and for all of us, who, unfortunately, find it so natural and comfortable to read the Bible subjectively.

The Neo-Pentecostal, often schooled in a neo-orthodox view of revelation, tends to bring that view to his handling of the Bible. In the neo-orthodox view revelation does not convey information at all but is the direct experience of God in a personal encounter.

Anyone trained in neo-orthodox theology (which some with good reason have called the "New Modernism") can easily embrace Pentecostalism because the two systems are so remarkably alike both in their distrust of rationality in religion and their emphasis on "experiencing God."

The subjective awareness in the following example illustrates this modern view of revelation:

> A young girl is sitting in the choir. Down in the auditorium is a young man, obviously interested in the girl. You watch with some amusement as she carefully studies her music, avoiding but feeling his gaze. Then, finally, she glances up and their eyes meet. She flushes slightly and looks away. But in that intense instant each communicated something of himself to the other. . . .
> Each of them is sure something exciting and tremendous has happened. Each of them *knows* that he shared something of himself, the intensity of his feelings, with the other. How? He knows because he experienced. It was real. He "knew" her and she "knew" him, in a way no mere words could express.[16]

There were no words; no information was given, yet they know something wonderful has happened. But how can they be sure? How does the young man know that she was thinking of him or even looking at him? Perhaps she was looking past him to someone else and thinking about the date she had with that other man the night before. The young man needs communication *in words*. And he needs to be sure he understands them in the sense the girl intended. When we seek to know God, it is essential for us to hear the words of God and to hear them in the sense God means them.

Larry Christenson, one of the first Protestant ministers to introduce Pentecostalism into his congregation, expresses a view of Christianity which has an obvious affinity with neo-orthodoxy:

> The Christian religion is essentially an experience—a personal experience of God. Theology and doctrine are simply an explanation of that experience. Many people know something about the doctrine, but have never really had the experience. So of course their religion is dry, formal, powerless. It has no life, no zest, no sense of reality.[17]

Christenson suggests a discipline to lift a person above his drab and lifeless religion and lead him into an exciting experience of God. It is a daily "quiet time with God." For the "quiet time" one needs a quiet place, a notebook, a pen, and a Bible. One is to read the Bible, says Christenson, not "simply to 'understand,' " but with a "feeling of 'openness' and 'receptivity' " (an effort to understand would get in the way of pure experience). He continues:

> Write down what comes to you during this reading-meditating-praying time . . . . When you write down, you begin to crystalize and capture the actual workings of the Holy Spirit in your heart, mind and soul. Make it quite personal and direct. Not simply what the passage "means," but what it means to and for you. Perhaps it will trigger some thought not directly related to the passage you are reading. That's all right. Write it down. This is the Holy Spirit's personal message to you.[18]

One of the easiest things in the world is to identify the inclinations of our own heart with an inner speaking of God. Unless we deliberately reject this approach, we shall be listening only to subjective answers (to our own thoughts). We shall be like the poor young man who looked up and thought he saw someone's eyes looking into his and built everything on that.

Contrary to Christenson, what we must do, if we respect the Bible as the word of God, is to understand what it says objectively—not what it means *to me* but what it *means*. Only when we have ascertained its meaning by careful, exacting study can we make any meaningful effort to apply it. This approach will require a study of Scripture in large segments rather than single texts in isolation.

Questions and Answers

1. Shouldn't we be hungry? Didn't Jesus say in the Sermon on the Mount: "Blessed are they that hunger and thirst after righteousness" (Matt. 5:6)?

Yes, he did, but he said also, " . . . for they shall be filled." When do you think they will be filled? How will they be filled? Should a person still feel thirsty after he comes to Christ? "Whosoever drinketh of the water that I shall give him," said Jesus, "shall never thirst" (John 4:14). A person's thirst is quenched by Christ. Being thirsty after drinking of Christ is not complimentary to him. "He that cometh to me shall not hunger, and he that believeth on me shall never thirst" (John 6:35). Thanksgiving is the proper response of the hungry and thirsty soul refreshed by him. This attitude, not a desperate sense of poverty, now motivates the Christian.

2. In Luke 11:13 what does it mean to ask for the Holy Spirit?

Could this mean that the *Christian* is to ask for the Spirit as if he had never been given? When, according to Paul, does one receive the Spirit? We receive the Spirit by hearing the gospel and believing it (Gal. 3:2). We thus begin our Christian life in the Spirit (Gal. 3:3). Since the Spirit comes with the hearing of the gospel, when we become Christians, would it be sensible for us to pray God to give us the Spirit as if we had never received him? If a friend has come to my home for a visit and has been there for a week, it would be ridiculous for me to go to the airport to meet him. Imagine me at the airport insisting, "I am going to wait for my friend until he comes." If I am a Christian, it would be equally absurd for me to pray for the coming of the Spirit. No Christian is ever recorded as praying to receive the Spirit.

David prayed, "Cast me not away from thy presence," and parallel to that, he asks, "Take not thy holy Spirit from me" (Psalm 51:11). In a similar way the Christian may pray that God will continue to be with him, or that he will continue to grant him his Spirit, or continue to have fellowship with him through his Spirit. That would be an appropriate Christian prayer. But for the Christian to pray "God, grant me the Spirit" would be quite improper, because he received the Spirit when he became a Christian, by the hearing of faith and at his baptism.

There is a proper way to ask God to grant the Spirit initially. Since the Spirit is promised in baptism (Acts 2:38, cf. I Cor. 12:13), that act is the correct way of asking for the Spirit. Baptism itself is a request to God for his blessings. It is, says the apostle Peter, an "appeal to God" (I Peter 3:21, R.S.V.).

3. What is the meaning of Ephesians 5:18: "be filled with the Spirit"? This is addressed to Christians.

"Be filled" (*plerousthe*) is present imperative, not aorist, and means "continue to be filled." It challenges Christians to continue, to persevere, in a present reality. It does not refer to an initial reception of the Spirit. Consult again Galatians 3:2 and 5: We receive the Spirit initially ("Received: in v. 2 is past) by the "hearing of faith"; God continues to supply ("supplieth" in v. 5 is present) the Spirit by the same means.

Questions to Guide Study

1. Read Colossians 2:9,10 and 2:16 in different translations. Note the way the tense is translated in 2:10 and the various ways "humility" (18,23) is rendered.
2. From the context of Ephesians 1:3 what blessings do you understand are included in "every spiritual blessing" "in Christ"?

3. Is Pentecostalism's view of the "full gospel" truly Christ-centered? Does the concept of the "full gospel" lessen the importance of the fact that he "died for our sins"? How important is that fact in the New Testament?
4. Explain the context of Ephesians 4:5. Can it permit the concept of two baptisms? If in the New Testament's one baptism we are given fulness, can there be any place for a second, higher baptism?
5. What is the Pentecostal means of receiving the Holy Spirit? Does the Pentecostal means differ from that presented in the New Testament?
6. Do you believe it is essential to study Biblical passages in their own context? Why? Can you illustrate the ill effect of removing passages from their context?
7. Is a preoccupation with miraculous gifts consistent with the New Testament's presentation of the Spirit's work?

---

[1] Lewi Pethrus, *The Wind Bloweth Where It Listeth: Thoughts and Experiences Concerning the Baptism of the Holy Spirit,* 2d ed. Tr. Harry Lindblom (Chicago: Philadelphia Book Concern, 1945), p. 20, cited in Bruner, p. 128, n. 15.

[2] Thomas B. Barratt, *When the Fire Fell,* p. 103, cited in Bruner, p. 121. (The emphasis is Barratt's).

[3] John H. Osteen, "Pentecost Is Not A Denomination: It Is An Experience," Full Gospel Business Men's Voice, 8 (June 1960), 4, cited in Bruner, p. 127.

[4] John G. Lake, "Dr. John G. Lake's Message on the Baptism of the Holy Spirit," *New Wine,* III, no. 11, 4.

[5] Ibid., p. 6.

[6] Ibid.

[7] Ibid.

[8] Ibid.

[9] Ibid., p. 7.

[10] Ibid., p. 5.

[11] Ibid., p. 6.

[12] Donald Gee, *Upon All Flesh: A Pentecostal World Tour* (Springfield, Mo.: Gospel Publishing House, 1935), p. 65, cited in Bruner, p. 107.

[13] Cited in Bruner, p. 263.

[14] Werner Skibstedt, *Die Geistestaufe im Licht der Bibel,* tr. and ed. Otto Witt (1946), p. 60, cited in Bruner, p. 114.

[15] Bruner, p. 265.

[16] Lawrence O. Richards, *Creative Bible Teaching* (Chicago: Moody Press, 1970), p. 21.

[17] Larry Christenson, *Speaking in Tongues* (Minneapolis: Bethany Fellowship, 1968), cited in *The Holy Spirit in Today's Church,* ed. Erling Jorstad (Nashville: Abingdon Press, 1973), p. 50.

[18] Ibid., p. 52.

CHAPTER X

The Holy Spirit in Acts:
Does Salvation Come in Stages?

The central Pentecostal thesis is that the Christian life is given in stages: there is a higher experience beyond conversion gained by the meeting of conditions beyond conversion, and on this subsequent experience one is taught to set his heart. One becomes a Christian and then with enough devotion and emptying and surrender and striving he reaches another, a far greater experience—an experience which is radiant, thrilling, life-giving and power-filling. After conversion, say Pentecostals, one is to seek the "baptism in the Holy Spirit" (their term for the reception of the Spirit) with the expectation of speaking in tongues as the initial evidence of the Spirit's full coming. One receives his "personal Pentecost" by "paying the price" of Pentecost.

Where, according to Pentecostalism, is this thesis supported? Is the subsequent experience documented in the gospels? No, Pentecostals answer, we find only promises of the experience in the gospels. In the epistles? No, we are told, because the epistles were written to people who already had the experience. "If we are to discover," says Brumback, "what definitely took place when one was baptized or filled with the Spirit in the early church, we must turn to the Book of Acts, the experience book of the New Testament Church. There alone can we find a detailed description of the baptism or filling with the Spirit which was experienced by those early believers."[1] By Pentecostal admission, this post-conversion experience, which is so important everyone should seek it, cannot be found in any epistle of the New Testament. "In the Book of Acts," explains Reed, "are found all instances of persons receiving the baptism in the Spirit which are to be found in the Bible.[2]

What evidence would be required from Acts to sustain the thesis? Support would have to be found for three elements. (1) A subsequent, higher experience must be established. (2) Conditions beyond conversion must be discovered. (3) Tongues must be shown to be *expected* as evidence of the experience. Are these elements really found in Acts?

The Meaning of Pentecost (Acts 2)

"And when the day of Pentecost was now come, they were all

88

together in one place. And suddenly there came from heaven a sound as of the rushing of a mighty wind, and it filled all the house where they were sitting" (vv. 1,2). They are not strenuously meeting the "conditions of Pentecost" either by "seeking," "yielding," or even praying. They are "sitting," waiting for God to act. And at the time of God's choosing "suddenly" "from heaven" the promised gift comes. With it there is the sound of a rushing, mighty wind. Pentecostals say there are some things about Pentecost which are not repeatable. One of them is the sound of the wind. We are told not to expect this.

"And there appeared unto them tongues parting asunder, like as of fire; and it sat upon each of them. And they were all filled with the Holy Spirit, and began to speak with other tongues, as the Spirit gave them utterance" (vv. 3,4). Here is another phenomenon we are told not to expect to be repeated—a tongue flickering like fire which sat upon each one of them as a visible symbol of the tongue each received. But the speaking in tongues is considered part of a repeatable "pattern" established at Pentecost. It is to be expected and sought as evidence of the Spirit's coming. Note, however, two things about their speaking in tongues. First, was the speaking in tongues sought or expected? So far as Luke records, it was not sought. It was totally unexpected. In fact, nowhere does Luke record a seeking of the "baptism in the Spirit" with the expectation of tongues as evidence. Second, the tongues were intelligible foreign languages. This is made clear in verses 5-11.

When Pentecostals say "Pentecost," what they mean is Acts 2:4. Pentecost means to them, not the preaching of Christ which was enabled by the Spirit, not the beginning of the church, not the forgiveness of sins which comes through Christ. When Pentecostals say "Pentecost," they mean one thing: the coming of the Spirit bringing power and tongues. But it must be observed that the experience of Acts 2 was not sought by meeting any conditions, and the tongues they received were not special "prayer languages" to be used in worship but foreign languages—a symbol of the world-wide mission of the church begun that day. These two facts call in question Acts 2:4 as a pattern for Pentecostalism.

Peter then explains (vv. 16-21) from Joel's prophecy of the outpouring of the Spirit what had happened, moving quickly to the reason for the Spirit's coming: "And it shall be, that whosoever shall call on the name of the Lord shall be saved" (v. 21). This is the thing which the outpouring of the Spirit is concerned with. The coming of the Spirit is not marveled at or relished for its own sake. The Spirit is interested in bringing men to call upon the name of the Lord and be saved. The coming of the Spirit was to inspire the sermon in which Christ is proclaimed and salvation is offered. In reality, Pentecostalism has misunderstood the purpose of the

89

Spirit's coming in Acts 2. It has missed what Acts 2 is designed to teach.

The apostle now begins his sermon: "Ye men of Israel, hear these words: Jesus of Nazareth . . . . (v. 22). That is the one he proceeds to talk about. He does not bring them a testimony of his experience in the Spirit. He does not begin by saying: "I want to tell you about this glorious experience I have had. You can have it, too, if you are willing to pay the price." Having explained in his introduction the purpose of the Spirit's coming, he turns now to his subject proper and soberly tells them who Jesus of Nazareth is.

"Let all the house of Israel therefore know assuredly, that God hath made him both Lord and Christ, this Jesus whom ye crucified" (v. 36). This is the thrust of Peter's sermon. Its purpose is to move men to faith in Jesus of Nazareth, who was crucified and raised again, and whom God had made Lord and Christ. When we think about Pentecost, what ought to come vividly to mind is the Spirit-inspired sermon in which Jesus is proclaimed as Lord and Messiah.

"Now when they heard this, they were pricked in their heart, and said unto Peter and the rest of the apostles, Brethren, what shall we do? And Peter said unto them, Repent ye, and be baptized every one of you in the name of Jesus Christ unto the remission of your sins; and ye shall receive the gift of the Holy Spirit" (vv. 37,38). The gift of the Spirit is placed precisely here at their conversion, when they came to Christ, not at some post-conversion experience. The whole of salvation is received at once: both the forgiveness of sins *and* the gift of the Holy Spirit. The pattern established at Pentecost does not indicate stages of salvation. Significant, too, is the use of the word "gift." The Spirit is not something for which one has "paid the price" or of which one has become worthy or deserving, but is received as a *gift* at baptism into Christ.

The Samaritans (Acts 8:14-17)

"Now when the apostles that were at Jerusalem heard that Samaria had received the word of God, they sent unto them Peter and John: who when they were come down, prayed for them, that they might receive the Holy Spirit; for as yet it was fallen upon none of them: only they had been baptized into the name of the Lord Jesus. Then laid they their hands on them, and they received the Holy Spirit." This is a key passage for the doctrine of subsequence. Let us examine it carefully. It should be observed first that the apostles cast no blame upon the Samaritans and imposed no further conditions on them for receiving the Spirit. What probing questions did the apostles ask the Samaritans? "Have you believed completely enough? Have you repented deeply enough? Have you prayed ardently enough to receive the Spirit?" They asked none of these things. What steps did they prescribe for them to receive the Spirit? None. The apostles discovered no fault in the Samaritan Christians. They had no exhortations for them to press on to another experience.

Two explanations have been given to the "Holy Spirit" of verses 15 and 17. (1) It is said to mean the Holy Spirit himself, and (2) it is taken by metonymy for the gifts of the Holy Spirit (for the metonymy cf. I Cor. 12:12: "so also is Christ" = the body of Christ). Even if the first interpretation is adopted, no real support is given to the doctrine of subsequent experience. The first view does not support the division of baptism and the Spirit; the text indicates rather that the Spirit and baptism belong together. The "not yet" shows that he was expected. It was considered abnormal for a believer to be baptized and "not yet" to have received the Spirit. "The Spirit *is* to come with baptism, but this coming had 'not yet' occurred. The relation of baptism to the Spirit, the 'not yet' indicates, is the relation of cohesion."[3] On the second interpretation, the "not yet," written from the perspective of Luke, looks to the gifts, which he knew were to come. This second explanation involves no subsequent reception of the Holy Spirit himself but only of gifts of the Spirit. That gifts of the Spirit are meant is suggested by the statement: "Now when Simon *saw* that through the laying on of the apostle's hands the Holy Spirit was given . . . ." (v. 18).

The two views (of the meaning of "Holy Spirit" in vv. 15,17) are united in their understanding of the reason for what happened. It will be helpful to remember that the events occurred in Samaria. For the first time the gospel has moved beyond Judaea to a non-Jewish people. It is perhaps difficult for us to realize the tensions between Jews and Samaritans. Long-standing ill will shows itself in John's report of Jesus' visit to Samaria: "The Samaritan woman therefore saith unto him, How is it that thou, being a Jew, askest drink of me, who am a Samaritan woman? (For Jews have no dealings with Samaritans)" (John 4:9). Enmity is apparent in the charge flung at Jesus: "Say we not well that thou art a Samaritan, and hast a demon" (John 8:48)?

Against this background the tremendous questions raised in Samaria are understandable. Can the despised Samaritans be admitted to the church of God as equals? Can they receive the Spirit of God along with their Jewish brethren? Will the Samaritans constitute an inferior sect or will they be received into the church on the same terms and stand on an equal footing with the Jews? Is the church indeed to be universal or are people to be barred because of race or previous religion? These are the crucial questions requiring answers at the critical juncture when the gospel moved out of Judaea into Samaria on its way into the remotest parts of the world (Acts 1:8). The answers needed to be heard by Samaritans and Jews and, as subsequent events prove, even by the apostle Peter.

What was done to answer these questions? Apostles, the most notable ones at that, Peter and John, were sent down to Samaria. When they came, they did not tell the Samaritans to agonize and yield completely, nor did they find any fault in them. The apostles (not the Samaritans) prayed, laid hands on them, and the Samaritans received outward, visible manifestations of the Spirit, in the sight of all, as a token of God's approval. The question has been answered: the Samaritans had become Christians and were to be received in equal standing with all who upon faith in Christ are baptized into him.

What particular gifts (or gift) from the Spirit the Samaritans received Luke does not indicate. Apparently he was not interested in the identity of the gifts but in the larger questions of the standing of the Samaritans and the nature of Christianity raised by the questions in Samaria. If Luke intends to teach that tongues are the initial evidence of the Spirit's coming, he passed by an excellent opportunity here.

On the view that "Holy Spirit" in verses 15 and 17 is the Spirit himself rather than gifts of the Spirit, the meaning is taken this way: a question mark was deliberately placed over the Samaritans. Have these people become Christians? The strange withholding of the Holy Spirit, always given in Christian baptism except in this single instance, was meant to be temporary. Its purpose was to raise the question of the Samaritans' standing and then to answer it decisively. So that no further question could arise, it was answered in the presence of the apostles with the Spirit being given through their hands.

On either view, the Samaritan incident does not teach that subsequence is normal. If the "Holy Spirit" is taken personally, the incident shows that subsequence is "an impossible contradiction in Christian realities."[4] If "Holy Spirit" stands for gifts of the Spirit, then there is no subsequence in the reception of the Spirit at all; it is only gifts that are subsequent. Furthermore, the apostles laid down no conditions beyond conversion. Speaking in tongues is not even mentioned.

The Case of Cornelius (Acts 10:34-11:18)

"Of a truth I perceive that God is no respecter of persons: but in every nation he that feareth him, and worketh righteousness, is acceptable to him" (vv. 34,35). The whole of Acts 10 should be examined to get the full impact of Peter's opening statement in his sermon at the house of Cornelius. To teach the apostle that God is not one to show partiality was the purpose of the vision in which the vessel was let down from heaven (10:9-16), but he was perplexed about its meaning (v. 17). Events which occurred immediately afterwards helped to clarify it (vv. 19-23). The precise moment when Peter discovered the significance of the vision is not clear, but by the time he reached the house of Cornelius he had grasped it: "Ye yourselves know," he said, "how it is an unlawful thing for a man that is a Jew to join himself or come unto one of another nation; and yet unto me hath God showed that I should not call any man common or unclean" (v. 28). If everyone had understood this impartiality of God and the Lordship of Christ over all men (v. 36), the unusual things which happened at the house of Cornelius would have been unnecessary. Unfortunately, not everyone understood what Peter had learned.

As Peter was explaining to the assembled group that, as all the prophets had taught, *everyone* (without exception, whether Jew or gentile) who believes in Christ receives the forgiveness of sins, the Holy Spirit fell upon all those who were listening to his message (vv. 43,44). "And they of the circumcision that believed were amazed, as many as came with Peter, because that on the Gentiles also was poured out the gift of the Holy Spirit. For they heard them speak with tongues and magnify God" (vv. 45,46). Peter does not say, "Since you have had the real experience, you do not need baptism in 'mere' water." He does not separate baptism and the Spirit; he joins them: "Can any man forbid the water, that these should not be baptized, who have received the Holy Spirit as well as we? And he commanded them to be baptized in the name of Jesus Christ" (vv. 47,48). When Peter thinks of comparing these events to something, he can think only of what happened on the day of Pentecost when Jews received the gift of the Holy Spirit and spoke in tongues. This was not something he had seen every day. The meaning the apostle sees in what occurred at the house of Cornelius is that surely no one can refuse them the water of baptism in which they will become the people of God. God wants gentiles as well as Jews to be Christians.

When Peter came up to Jerusalem, the circumcision party took issue with him because he had gone into the house of uncircumcised men and, worse than that, had actually eaten with them. How could he (vv. 1-3)? Here we get a sense of the deep need for the lesson of Caesarea which these men had yet to learn. The apostle then explained to them what had happened (vv. 4-17). "And as I began to speak," he tells them, "the Holy Spirit fell on them, even as on us at the beginning. And I remembered the word of the Lord, how he said, John indeed baptized with water; but ye shall be baptized in the Holy Spirit" (vv. 15,16). He does not say, "The Holy Spirit fell on them evidenced by tongues as he always does on everyone." He knows only one thing with which to compare it: what happened on Pentecost. "If then God gave unto them the like gift as he did also unto us, when we believed on the Lord Jesus Christ, who was I, that I could withstand God" (v. 17)? The granting of the Spirit to the gentiles made it obvious to Peter that God wanted them as his people. For him to refuse them baptism and entrance to God's kingdom would have meant trying to undo the purpose of God.

"And when they heard these things, they held their peace, and glorified God, saying, Then to the Gentiles also hath God granted repentance unto life" (v. 18). That is the meaning of what happened at the house of Cornelius. Even the most stubborn understood it. God intended to include gentiles among his people.

Among the events at Caesarea, where is the doctrine of subsequence? It clearly is not present. The only way subsequence could be introduced is to maintain that Cornelius was a Christian before Peter came to him. But this is impossible (Acts 11:14). Where is the meeting of conditions beyond conversion to receive the Spirit? There are no such conditions. To be sure, tongues are present as at Pentecost, but where is the seeking? Where is the *expectation* of tongues as evidence of the Spirit? Where is the granting of the gift to only the few who have "paid the price of Pentecost"? The apostle gave Cornelius no instruction in how to seek the Spirit. He did not teach him to expect tongues as the first manifestation of the Spirit. The absence of subsequence and of seeking along with the fact that tongues were not expected means the absence of the Pentecostal "pattern."

Paul's Message to Christians (Acts 14:22,23)

After Paul and Barnabas had made many disciples in Antioch, Iconium, and Lystra, they returned to those cities (Acts 14:21), "confirming [strengthening] the souls of the disciples, exhorting them to continue in the faith, and that through many tribulations we must enter into the kingdom of God. And when they had appointed for them elders in every church, and had prayed with fasting, they commended them to the Lord, on whom they had believed." As the first message intended for Christians we have encountered, this passage takes on special significance. The reader of Acts knows that in speaking to pagans Paul began with the nature of God (Acts 14:11-17, 17:16-31). To those who already knew the one God he proclaimed Christ. But what did he preach to Christians? If he taught that salvation comes in stages, that there is a higher experience which brings power for life and service to be sought after justification, we should expect to hear it at this point.

Try to imagine Paul's efforts to strengthen the recently-converted disciples this way: "You have made a start, but do you have all the power you want? Do you have all the joy you want? Do you want to rise above the humdrum and monotony of your present life into the life of full victory? Because testimonies have power to draw men to the work of the Spirit, I want you to hear the testimony of brother Barnabas. He will share with you something wonderful that has happened in his life." Is this the Paul who said "in him ye are made full" (Col. 2:10)?

Instead of an airy dream world what Paul brings them is genuine and substantial. His strengthening message is: "continue in the faith," the same faith you were taught in the beginning and which made you Christians. Paul knows of nothing "higher" than faith in Christ. And, he continues honestly, "Through many tribulations we must enter into the kingdom of God." In Paul's presentation of Christianity there is at the beginning faith and at the end the heavenly kingdom. Between them are many difficulties, not a higher blessing. His exhortation is to persevere in faith through the obstacles. He does not promise so much power that problems no longer seem to be problems. As part of the strengthening effort they appointed elders in every church. And, finally, they entrusted the disciples to the care of the Lord in whom they had believed.

The Ephesian Disciples (Acts 19:1-7)

> And it came to pass, that, while Apollos was at Corinth, Paul having passed through the upper country came to Ephesus, and found certain disciples: and he said unto them, Did ye receive the Holy Spirit when ye believed? And they said unto him, Nay, we did not so much as hear whether the Holy Spirit was given. And he said, Into what then were ye baptized? And they said, Into John's baptism. And Paul said, John baptized with the baptism of repentance, saying unto the people that they should believe on him that should come after him, that is, on Jesus. And when they heard this, they were baptized into the name of the Lord Jesus. And when Paul had laid his hands upon them, the Holy Spirit came on them; and they spake with tongues, and prophesied. And they were in all about twelve men.

Pentecostalism regards this passage as a basic support for its doctrine of subsequence. But instead of teaching a coming of the Spirit following conversion as a separate work of grace, it teaches the one and only coming of the Spirit at conversion. It teaches clearly the union of faith, baptism, and the Spirit.

Why Paul suspected that the disciples had not received the Spirit Luke does not report. He certainly does not reveal that Paul had doubts because, as has been suggested, he observed their drab, powerless lives. The only reason for his suspicion intimated in the context is the activity of Apollos, who lacked an understanding of Christian baptism, in which the Spirit is given (Acts 18:24-26).

Paul's first question (v. 2) to the Ephesians is: "Did ye receive the Holy Spirit when ye believed" (*pisteusantes,* ingressive aorist = when you became believers)? The question indicates that Paul expected the Spirit to come with faith in Christ. As he taught the Galatians, the Spirit is received "by the hearing of faith" in the beginning (Gal. 3:2,3, cf. John 7:37-39). Instead of teaching subsequence Paul's question leaves no place for it.

We should observe what questions Paul does not raise. He does not ask, "Do you know that after conversion you are not to be satisfied until you have received the fulness of God's blessings? Were you taught that you are incomplete until you receive the subsequent experience of the Spirit? Has your faith become complete? Have you yielded totally, removed all known sin, and prayed earnestly enough?" Nor does he ask, "Who laid hands on you to impart the Spirit to you?"

Paul's second question is simply: "Into what then were ye baptized" (v. 3)? His questions ("Did ye receive the Holy Spirit when ye believed?" and "Into what then were ye baptized?") indicate that baptism is the place where faith is given concrete expression and the Spirit is received (cf. Acts 2:38). Their problem was their baptism, for they had received only John's baptism, in which the Spirit is not given. Paul then explained that John's baptism meant faith not in Jesus but only in the promised Messiah (v. 4). The Ephesian disciples had never come to believe in Jesus of Nazareth as the Christ; they had believed only in the Messiah who was to come. They had never before realized the personal identity of the Messiah. When they understood this, for the first time, "they were baptized into the name of the Lord Jesus" (v. 5). What we have is not a subsequent Christian experience. The Ephesians are not going beyond their Christian beginning, but only now do they become Christians on the occasion of their baptism into Christ.

And when Paul had laid his hands upon them, the Holy Spirit came on them; and they spake with tongues, and prophesied" (v. 6). Paul does not teach the necessity of the laying on of hands for the reception of the Spirit. What he teaches is faith in Christ and baptism. Neither does he teach the necessity of tongues, nor that tongues are to be expected as evidence. While it is interesting that the Ephesians spoke in tongues, it does not fit the Pentecostal pattern. None of the necessary elements is present—neither conditions beyond conversion, nor expectation of tongues taught to the recipients of the Spirit. Note that speaking in tongues and prophesying were given to all twelve disciples. Three instances of speaking in tongues are recorded in Acts (2:4, 10:44-46, 19:1-7). In no case are conditions laid down for receiving the gift, in no case are Christians taught not to be satisfied with their completeness until they have spoken in tongues, in no case are tongues said to be expected or required as proof of the Spirit's coming. In every instance tongues are given to an entire group, not to single individuals who are ardently seeking the Spirit.

Paul's Second Message to Christians (Acts 20:17-38)

At Miletus Paul reminds the Ephesian elders that he had not shrunk from declaring "anything that was profitable" (v. 20) and that he had declared "the whole counsel of God" (v. 27). He summarizes his teaching as a message of "repentance toward God, and faith toward our Lord Jesus Christ" (v. 21) and characterizes his preaching as testifying "the gospel of the grace of God" (v. 24). His summary includes no second, higher experience. He taught no such experience during his three year stay in Ephesus, nor does he offer them one now as a protection against the "grievous wolves" which threatened to invade them. What he presents for their strengthening is the same message by which they had begun as Christians: "And now I commend you to God, and to the word of his grace, which is able to build you up, and to give you the inheritance among all them that are sanctified" (v. 32). The "word of his grace" itself has power (*dunameno*) "to build up" and "give the inheritance." How can there be need for a deeper, subsequent work of God to grant power for life and service? Does the "word of his grace" need supplementing?

Conclusion

Acts does not teach that salvation is given in stages. Salvation is one organic whole, given all at once. The very passages in Acts which are supposed to teach a second work of grace, in fact teach only one. Acts does not teach that the coming of the Spirit must be accompanied by extraordinary signs. At certain critical junctures in Acts, for good reasons, there were miraculous events. But the norm is the quiet and simple conversion.

Questions and Answers

1. **Explain the difference in the Holy Spirit we receive when we are baptized and the baptism of the Holy Spirit with which the apostles were able to give the power of miraculous gifts to people.**

The same Holy Spirit who was present with the apostles is present also with us. The difference is not in the Holy Spirit, who as Deity, is forever the same unchanging person. Nor does the difference consist in the "amount" of the Holy Spirit given. The Spirit is a Person, not an impersonal force or physical substance;

when he is present therefore, he is present as a person—that is, fully. The difference, rather, is the work the Spirit comes to do. My colleague, Dr. Marlin Connelly, illustrates the point by comparing it to the work of a contractor. The contractor may undertake many different tasks: he may build now a school, now a house, at another time a factory or a hospital, but he is the same contractor.

The Holy Spirit came to the apostles to qualify them as authoritative, inerrant teachers of Christ: the Spirit causes them to remember and understand what Jesus had taught them (John 14:26); he thereby guaranteed the authenticity of the apostles' testimony about Christ (John 15:26,27). The Spirit worked in the apostles, not only to qualify them as messengers of Christ, but also to demonstrate the fact that they were authoritative, specially accredited messengers. Hence, he did special signs through them (II Cor. 12:12).

The Holy Spirit uses his work in the apostles to convict us of sin, righteousness, and judgment and to bring us to faith in Christ (John 16:8-11). He then dwells in us to encourage (I Cor. 6:19,20) and to strengthen us in living the Christian life (Rom. 8:13).

2. **The fact that the apostles and the Samaritans knew that the Holy Spirit had not been given to them is an indication that there was always an outward sign—some way of knowing that the Holy Spirit had been given. Why is there no outward sign today?**

If there was always an outward sign, what does Luke indicate that it was? Certainly there were special manifestations of the Spirit at times, but have we not seen good reasons for them in the instances we have examined? Is the reason not obvious in the case of the Samaritans (Acts 8:14-17)? And in the case of the gentiles (Acts 10:44-48)? Could we say that Luke indicates that there were extraordinary manifestations every time the Spirit came? God has promised the Spirit at baptism, but has he promised to give everyone a special sign? Of course, if the "Holy Spirit" in Acts 8:15 and 17 means the gifts of the Spirit, then there is no problem about their knowing the gifts had not come.

Consider the following points:

(1) All Christians have the Spirit (Rom. 8:9). Therefore, the same evidence that shows one is a Christian shows also that he has the Spirit.

(2) Acts 8:26-39, the conversion of the Ethiopian eunuch, is a normal case of conversion. Beginning with Isaiah 53, Philip brought good news to him about Jesus. As they rode along, they came to a certain water, and the eunuch asked whether he could be baptized. Philip immediately baptized him, and the eunuch "went on his way rejoicing" (v. 39). Did the eunuch become a Christian?

He certainly did. Why do we say so? Because the gospel was preached to him, he believed it and was baptized into Christ. Did he receive the Spirit? Yes. How do we know? Receiving the Spirit is synonymous with becoming a Christian. The two are not meant to be separated. Luke gives no extraordinary sign. He says the eunuch "went on his way rejoicing." Why did he rejoice? Because he had become a Christian, with all that implies, including the gift of the Holy Spirit.

(3) We should not see the Spirit only in the extraordinary and spectacular. The Spirit of God should be seen in such ordinary things as faith in Christ, the act of baptism, a person's conviction of the love of God (Rom. 5:5), and rejoicing in the forgiveness of sins.

(4) Luke, after all, does give an outward sign of the Spirit's coming. It is not spectacular, but it is nonetheless real. The outward sign is baptism into Christ.

Questions to Guide Study

1. What is the primary Pentecostal thesis? Where do Pentecostals contend this thesis is supported? For what elements would we need proof to sustain the thesis? Is the proof really found in Acts?
2. What is the chief emphasis in Peter's sermon preached on Pentecost?
3. What is the purpose of the Spirit's coming on Pentecost?
4. What kind of questions would have arisen in Jewish and Samaritan minds when the Samaritans became Christians? How were these questions answered?
5. What is the meaning of the fact that Cornelius received the Spirit before his baptism? Did that make his baptism unnecessary?
6. What did Peter preach at the house of Cornelius? Was the Spirit the content of his sermon?
7. What message did Paul preach to Christians? What at Lystra, Iconium, and Antioch? What to the Ephesian elders?
8. What were Paul's questions to the disciples at Ephesus? What do his questions indicate about the relationship between faith, baptism, and the Spirit?

---

[1] Carl Brumback, *What Meaneth This? A Pentecostal Answer to a Pentecostal Question* (Springfield, Mo.: Gospel Publishing House, 1947), p. 185.
[2] Glenn A. Reed, "Pentecostal Truths 322," Mimeographed Notes to a Course Taught at Central Bible Institute, Springfield, Mo., 1952-54, cited in Bruner, p. 61.
[3] Bruner, p. 177.
[4] Ibid.

CHAPTER XI

I Corinthians 12, 13, 14:
What Are the Marks of Spirituality?

Paul's subject in I Corinthians 12, 13, and 14 is the marks of spirituality ("Gifts" in 12:1 is not present in the Greek text; instead of "gifts" we could have either "things" or "men"). Paul apparently is replying to a question raised by the Corinthians: How does one recognize spirituality? Or, who is a spiritual person—that is, a person influenced by the Spirit of God? In the background of chapters 12 and 13 is the question of tongues: is the gift of tongues the supreme manifestation of the Spirit? The abuse of tongues is brought into the foreground in chapter 14.

The Corinthians' pagan past had not prepared them to recognize the working of God's Spirit. Their religion had been non-rational and ecstatic. With them, as with the modern Pentecostals, the highest religious expression consisted in being swept away in an inexplicable ecstatic experience. "You know how, in the days when you were still pagan, you were swept off to those dumb heathen gods, however you happened to be led" (12:2, N.E.B.). Pagan rituals were designed to induce ecstasy. The second century work by Apuleius describes such an ecstatic experience. It occurred when he was initiated into the mysteries of Isis.

> I approached near unto hell [*confinium mortis*], even to the gates of Proserpine, and after that I was ravished throughout all the elements, I returned to my proper place: about midnight I saw the sun brightly shine, I saw likewise the gods celestial and the gods infernal, before whom I presented myself and worshipped them.[1]

A young woman from Ghana, a Bible correspondence student, raises in a letter a question strikingly similar to the one dealt with by Paul in these chapters. She says that there are very many "spiritual churches" in Ghana. She has visited them on occasion, though she herself is not a member. She wants to know whether it is "true that when the Holy Spirit comes upon you, you behave like a mad person." She describes her observation in this way:

> When the pastor, the prophet, or the prophetess has prayed for some time, it will come to a time and you will see almost all the people talking something different.

100

When they finish and you ask them what they have said, they just tell you they don't know. Some even go to the extent of rolling themselves on the ground and so on and so forth. Then later they tell you the Holy Spirit descended on them.

She concludes with the question: "Is that how the Holy Spirit works?"

Does the Spirit manifest his presence by causing one to act like a "mad person"—that is, is the sign of his presence ecstasy? Does the Spirit manifest himself by lifting people above the ordinary and earthly, or by bringing the will of God into the ordinary and earthly? Is he recognized by the transport of emotion or by attention to everyday, human duties? How does the Spirit cause one to act? What are the distinguishing marks of the spiritual person?

(1) **The Spirit's Influence Is Evident in the Thoughtful Confession of Jesus as Lord** (I Cor. 12:3)

"No man can say, Jesus is Lord, but in the Holy Spirit." The evidence of the Spirit's influence is not, of course, the mere passing of the words "Jesus is Lord" through the lips (Matt. 7:21) but the confession thoughtfully and meaningfully made. "Lord" (*kurios*) in this confession is used not in the sense merely of "sir" (as in John 4:15,19) or of "master" as the correlative of slave (as in Luke 16:3,5,8) but in the high sense of John 1:1: "In the beginning was the Word, and the Word was with God, and the Word was God." When anyone says "Jesus is Lord," understands what he is saying and means the words, his confession is evidence that he is being influenced by God's Spirit. Such a person is being drawn by God to Christ, as he is taught by Scripture who Christ is and what he has done (John 6:44,45).

Evidence of the Spirit's influence is not making sounds that neither the speaker nor anyone else can understand. It is saying with understanding and meaning the simple and profound words: "Jesus is Lord." Intelligible, meaningful speech is the sign of the Spirit. Verses 2 and 3 make the point as strongly as it can be made that the ecstatic is not the evidence of the Spirit. Why would anyone ever get the idea that it is an unintelligible utterance which indicates the presence of the Spirit of God? Why would non-rationality be an indication of his presence? What could agree more with the Spirit's work than a thoughtful, meaningful confession of Jesus as Lord (John 16:8-11,14; cf. I John 4:2,3)?

(2) **The Spirit Manifests Himself not in One Particular Gift but in the Helpful Use of Whatever Gift One Has** (I Cor. 12:4-31)

Paul wants to broaden the narrow view of spirituality held by the

101

Corinthians, who thought the Spirit was shown supremely in one way and by means of one gift—tongues. The Corinthians evidently felt that speaking in tongues was evidence of a higher spirituality. Paul answers by laying down the principle, widely applicable, that there is more than one way to show the presence and influence of God's Spirit. It is apparent from the space devoted to this point that Paul regarded it as weighty.

Two words are emphasized throughout verses 4-11: "diversities" and "same." There is a wide variety of gifts and services and workings but the "same Spirit," the "same Lord" and the "same God" grant them. The various gifts are given not in recognition of the superior devotion or standing of the recipients but by the "one and the same Spirit," who gives to each one "as he will" (12:11). No one gift is given to all. It is obvious that one can have the Spirit and not speak in tongues (12:10, cf. 12:30).

In the next section (12:12-31) the two words stressed are "one" and "many"; "one" body and "many" functions (based on many gifts). The outward, observable act of baptism, in which all received the Spirit, shows the oneness of Christ's body (12:13). As the human body has many members with different functions, so does the body of Christ. If every member had the same function (because each had an identical gift), this one function could no more constitute a body than could one monstrous eye (12:17). The very concept "body" means that there are many members with different functions working together for the good of the whole.

Those in Corinth who made tongues the mark of superior spirituality fostered pride in themselves and left others with a sense of inferiority. Some had been made to feel so inferior that they questioned whether they had any place in the body at all while others were proud of their super-spirituality. On the contrary, Paul contends, the gifts do not indicate degrees of spirituality. They are purely functional. No member, then, should feel inferior (12:15,16), and none should feel superior (12:21). Paul dramatically represents the foot and the ear, suffering from their sense of inferiority, as doubting their membership in the body. If they could only be a hand or an eye, they could feel important! The eye and the head, in their great pride, doubt the place of the hand and foot in the body. They should all know that each has a vital place in the body and that their differences are indispensable for its well-being.

As a further illustration of this point, consider the fact that Dorcas had the gift of making clothing (Acts 9:36,39). If she had had the spirit of the foot and ear, she would have bewailed her lot somewhat like this: "All I can do is sew and help poor people. I wish I could do something really important and spiritual." If she had had the superior outlook of the eye or the head, she would have said: "I wonder why no one else cares. I am the only one serving the Lord.''

Barnabas had the gift of encouraging (Acts 4:36). If he had been suffering from the inferiority complex of the foot and ear, he would have said: "There is no vital contribution I can make." With the outlook of the eye or head, he would have looked from his superior height on all others and asked: "Why will someone besides me not take his responsibility seriously? Why does the Lord have no real servant but me?"

I Corinthians 12 deals with extraordinary gifts; the problem was that some in Corinth were making tongues evidence of a higher spirituality. The passages in Acts deal with non-miraculous talents. But the principle is identical. It is a principle easy to neglect.

(3) The Spirit of God is Shown in Love (I Cor. 13)

In the first section (vv. 1-3) Paul says that no gift a person can have, whether tongues or prophecy or knowledge miraculously imparted or miracle-working faith has any value without love. A person may exhibit any or all of these gifts and not be spiritual. A person with love and no extraordinary gift at all is spiritual. No gift at all, no act at all, without love, is spiritual. Love, Paul wants the Corinthians to know, is a manifestation of the Spirit superior to tongues and to all other gifts. It is the more "excellent way" (12:31).

A little boy wanted to do something for his father. "Is there anything I can do for you?" he asked. His father, trying hard to think of something, said, "Yes, you can bring me a glass of water." The lad had been playing outside and his hands were dirty. As he held the glass, a finger accidentally stuck into the water and left a cloudy trail. Do you think the father drank the water? Of course he did. The smallest thing done with love is meaningful. The most spectacular and impressive thing without love is nothing.

The second section (vv. 4-7) presents the characteristics of love. Love is not shown in explosive emotion but in the control of emotion: it is patient and kind, is not arrogant or selfish. Negatively, it avoids doing harm. Positively, it seeks to do good.

The third section (vv. 8-13) stresses the fact that love is permanent while all miraculous gifts are only temporary. "Love never faileth: but whether there be prophecies, they shall be done away; whether there be tongues, they shall cease; whether there be knowledge, it shall be done away" (v. 8). Paul's point is that one should be occupied with developing love rather than acquiring an impermanent gift. The effect is strongly to discourage the desire to speak in tongues. Aspiration should be directed to things which persist. "Now abideth faith, hope, love, these three" (v. 13).

(4) The Spirit Works in Conjunction with the Mind, not at a "Deeper" Level than the Mind, not in Bypassing the Mind (I Cor. 14:20)

"Brethren, be not children in mind: yet in malice be ye babes, but in mind be men." Similarly Jesus said: "Be ye therefore wise as serpents, and harmless as doves" (Matt. 10:16). We do not learn from Scripture to approach God in our "spirit" rather than our "mind," as if our "spirit" constituted a deeper level of communication with God than our "mind." The Biblical view of man does not divide man in this way. It does not distinguish "spirit" and "mind" as separate faculties of man. In the Biblical view of man whatever we do, we do as total persons. When we love God, we love him with the whole person, including our minds: "Thou shalt love the Lord thy God with all thy heart, and with all thy strength, and with all thy mind" (Luke 10:27). The Biblical emphasis is quite different from that of the anti-intellectual who says: "Whenever I go to church, I feel like unscrewing my head and placing it under the seat, because in a religious meeting I never have any use for anything above my collar button."[2]

True spirituality is not anti-intellectual. On the contrary, it requires a vigorous use of the mind. Throughout this chapter Paul stresses the need for thoughtful words which can be grasped with the mind. Without such intelligibility no edification can take place. Unless rational content is presented to the mind, people are only being manipulated on the basis of their feelings. It is necessary even for lifeless instruments to give a clear distinction in sounds so that it can be recognized what is being "piped or harped" (14:7). "If the trumpet give an uncertain voice, who shall prepare himself for war" (v. 8)? Paul applies his illustration in this way: "So also ye, unless ye utter by the tongue speech easy to be understood, how shall it be known what is spoken? for ye will be speaking into the air" (v. 9). Because all true worship requires the use of the mind, Paul insists: "What is it then"? "I will pray with the spirit, and I will pray with the understanding also" (v. 15). Even the ungifted person should be able to understand: "Else if thou bless with the spirit, how shall he that filleth the place of the unlearned say the Amen at thy giving of thanks, seeing he knoweth not what thou sayest" (v. 16)?

If the intellect is rejected, one has no protection against any kind of delusion that presents itself. "Beloved, believe not every spirit, but prove the spirits, whether they are of God. . . . Hereby know ye the Spirit of God: every spirit that confesseth that Jesus Christ is come in the flesh is of God" (I John 4:1,2). The test of the spirits is true doctrine about Christ—doctrine which can be judged only by the mind. If one chooses to bypass the mind, one is left only with the intensity of the emotional experience which the spirit brings as a test of genuineness ("It must be real because of the way it made me weep." "I know it is true because it gave me a wonderful sense of wholeness").

Disparaging the mind in the interest of a "higher spirituality" is widespread. Sometimes in an effort to be "spiritual" people ask the Holy Spirit which sock to put on first in the morning or what to prepare for dinner. Because of his non-rational view of spirituality, a person felt it would be unspiritual to rely on a watch rather than the Spirit. The person would leave his watch at home and look to the Spirit to nudge him or otherwise give him an awareness of the time when he was supposed to be present somewhere. Using the common sense which God gave us is rejected as unspiritual. Spirituality in life is regarded as a mechanical control by the Spirit. Spiritual worship is thought of as approaching God at a "deeper level" than the mind. Thus the Neo-Pentecostal Christenson praises speaking in tongues precisely because it "bypasses the mind."[3]

John Sherrill, reporting his journey into Neo-Pentecostalism, recalls that the "key" to his change was learning to distrust the mind in religion and to elevate experience to first place. Anxious about a scheduled operation for cancer, he went into a noonday Lenten meditation where he heard a young seminary student say that the problem of Nicodemus was that he was trying to approach Christ "through logic" (John 3:2; contrast John 20:30, 31 with the view of the seminarian).

> Many of us try, he said, to approach Christ as Nicodemus did: through logic. "Rabbi, we know that you are a teacher sent by God," Nicodemus said, and then he gave his reason—a logical one: " . . . no one could perform these signs of yours unless God were with him."
>
> "But, you see," said the seminarian, "as long as Nicodemus was trying to come to an understanding of Christ through his logic, he could never succeed. It isn't logic, but an experience, that lets us know who Christ is."[4]

The next morning he heard Catherine Marshall LeSourd say to him: "You're trying to approach Christianity through your mind, John . . . It simply can't be done that way."[5] Driving home, he turned to his wife and said: "What do they call it: 'a leap of faith'? All right, I'm going to make a leap: I believe that Christ was God."[6] Sherrill explains that it was "a cold-blooded laying down of my sense of what was logical, quite without emotional conviction."[7] Instead of a leap in the dark, with no intellectual underpinnings, Biblical faith is trusting what we are convinced is true. It is a conviction which involves a knowledge of content.

And they that know thy name will put their trust in thee;

For thou, O Lord, hast not forsaken them that seek thee (Psalm 9:10).

(5) The Spirit Promotes Respect for Scripture (I Cor. 14:37)

"If any man thinketh himself to be a prophet,. or spiritual, let him take knowledge of the things which I write unto you, that they are the commandment of the Lord." The implication for our day is that the spiritual person respects Scripture as the word of God. The spiritual person is not recognized by his claims of stirring visions and revelations. Claims of private conferences with the Spirit in which the will of God is revealed do not indicate spirituality. True spirituality is evidenced by adherence to apostolic testimony recorded for all generations in holy Scripture.

Quote Scripture to the "spiritually superior" person and he may answer, "I used to be on that level. I used to read Scripture on that literal level, but now I know the Spirit." The statement implies that he has direct communication with the Spirit and that the Spirit may tell him something different from the written word or give him some insight that a person could not get simply by reading Scripture and learning what it means in its context. A child sometimes tries to set his mother and father in opposition to each other. He goes to his mother and asks, "May I do this?" His mother says, "Ask your father." A wise father always asks, "What did your mother tell you?" Sometimes people try to get the Spirit to tell them something directly that he has not told them in the word. But if it were possible to have a private conference with the Spirit in which one inquired about the will of God, the Spirit would only refer the person to the word. From the word to the Spirit there can be no appeal. A person led by God's Spirit understands this.

What is Paul's test of a person led by the Spirit? It is his respect for Scripture. Honoring the Spirit means honoring Scripture as the word of God. This is so because Scripture is the word the Spirit has spoken and continues to speak. Whoever casts reflection on Scripture, minimizes or disparages it, gives sure proof that he is not under the influence of the Holy Spirit. The apostle John emphasizes the same point. "We are of God: he that knoweth God heareth us; he who is not of God heareth us not. By this view we know the spirit of truth, and the spirit of error" (I John 4:6).

(6) The Spirit Brings Order and Decorum (I Cor. 14:40)

"But let all things be done decently and in order." The spiritual person reflects the beauty of God's order in thought, worship, and life. Paul gives two reasons why the congregational meeting should be conducted with decency and order. The first is a practical reason: edification requires a thoughtful atmosphere, free from confusion. The second reason is a more profound one: disorder is the antithesis of God's nature.

106

It befit the character of Dionysus that his ancient worshipers worked themselves into an ecstatic frenzy. Why is this type of worship inappropriate in serving God? For the profound reason that "God is not a God of confusion, but of peace" (I Cor. 14:33). If one goes into a meeting where there is confusion, he comes away with certain impressions about the nature of the god the people worship. If people act irrationally in worship, the god they worship must be perceived to be irrational. In Christian worship, however, we come before God conscious of his nature as the God of order and reflect his nature in worship. We worship him meaningfully because he is the God of meaning, not of chaos. We misrepresent the God of Biblical revelation if we convey the impression that he is a God of disorder. What kind of god is being imagined when anyone thinks he can best approach him if he takes off his head?

Because God is the God of order, the prophet, moved to speak by God's Spirit, can control himself (14:32). If a prophet goes into a frenzy and says, "I cannot control myself because I am inspired by the Spirit," it is clear that he is not speaking by the Spirit of God. The meaningful, thoughtful, rational worship by people made in the image of God befits the nature of the God of order and peace.

Questions and Answers

Could tongues be the language of angels (I Cor. 13:1)?

First, Paul does not say that he or anyone else ever spoke in the tongues of angels, but what he says is that even "if" he had the gift of speaking all the languages in the world (human and angelic), but did not have love, it would only be so much noise. Second, whenever angels are recorded as speaking to men, their speech is always intelligible (I Kings 19:7, Acts 5:19,20, 12:7). Third, if tongues are the language of angels, we have something quite odd: the "tongue" of every tongues-speaker is different. Does that mean that every angel has his own special language? Fourth, if tongues are the language of angels, when tongues "cease" (I Cor. 13:8; according to glossolalists they cease when Christ returns), will the language of angels cease? Will they then be unable to communicate? Fifth, if Pentecost is the pattern for modern tongues-speaking, the tongues must be intelligible foreign languages currently spoken (Acts 2:4-11).

Questions to Guide Study

1. How would you answer the question of the young Ghanaian woman: Does the Spirit make one behave like a "mad person"?

2. From what kind of religious background had the Corinthians come? Did this prepare them to understand the working of God's Spirit?
3. Does the thoughtful confession of Jesus as a mark of the spiritual person harmonize with the Spirit's purpose? How?
4. In Corinth was there any one gift which was granted to everyone? How does Paul show this was not desirable? Can you apply his answer to our day?
5. Did every Christian in Corinth have the Spirit? Should everyone of them have expected to speak in tongues?
6. Can you see any danger in the view that the higher spirituality bypasses the mind? Why?
7. What does John Sherrill say was the key to his accepting Neo-Pentecostalism?
8. Is the spiritual person someone who has risen above the need for Scripture?
9. Why does the worship of God require order?

---

[1] Apuleius, *The Golden Ass: Being the Metamorphoses of Lucius Apuleius* xi. 23, tr. W. Adlington, rev. S Gaselee ("Loeb Classical Library"; New York: Macmillan, 1915).

[2] John R. W. Stott, *Your Mind Matters: The Place of the Mind in the Christian Life* (Downers Grove: Intervarsity Press, 1972) p. 30.

[3] Christenson, *Speaking in Tongues,* cited in Jorstad, p. 88.

[4] John L. Sherrill, *They Speak with Other Tongues* (Westwood, N. J.: Revell, 1964), pp. 9, 10.

[5] Ibid., p. 11.

[6] Ibid.

[7] Ibid.

CHAPTER XII

What About Glossolalia?

How should glossolalia be evaluated? (Glossolalia is the technical term for speaking in tongues. It is derived from the two Greek words *glossa,* "tongue," "language" and *lalein,* "to speak"). Is there solid evidence that real languages are being spoken? Does the "gift of interpretation" provide such evidence? If no real language is being spoken, is the experience Biblical? Should anyone seek the experience?

The Basis of Modern Glossolalia

Modern glossolalia is based on serious doctrinal error. Its central thesis contains these elements: (1) Christian fulness comes only with the reception of the Spirit after conversion. (2) Speaking in tongues is the initial evidence of the Spirit. (3) Every Christian should ardently seek the Spirit with the expectation of speaking in tongues. These views must be rejected for the following reasons.

(1) Fulness is in Christ (Col. 2:10). The possession of the Spirit is simply a result of being in Christ, is a part of Christian fulness, and is given at conversion (Eph. 1:3,14, Gal. 3:1,5, Acts 2:38). Dividing Christians into those who have only Christ and those who have the Spirit in addition to Christ by a separate act of faith disparages Christ and the efficacy of his redemptive work. This "full gospel" relocates the New Testament emphasis—away from the cross to an experience. This is the most serious error of the tongues movement.

(2) Tongues-speaking in Acts was not given as evidence to individuals of a higher experience but, as we have seen, served a larger purpose. Tongues were given at critical, unique junctures in the progress of the gospel. The gift indicated the approval of God on the course of events. On Pentecost the tongues were one of three miracles (along with the wind and fire) which marked the beginning of a new age and drew men together to hear the gospel (Acts 2:2-13). With the tongues at Caesarea God sanctioned the inclusion of the gentiles (Acts 10:44-11:18). At Ephesus tongues marked the end of the ministry of John the Baptist (Acts 19:1-7). In Acts tongues were given to entire groups, not to seeking individuals, and were intelligible languages in current use (Acts 2:6-11). There were signs of the Spirit other than tongues (e.g. Acts 2:2-4). Nowhere does the Bible say that speaking in tongues is the initial evidence of

the Spirit's coming, nor can it be inferred from anything Scripture does say. There is no indication in Acts that tongues are to be regarded as permanent. Many passages speak of the coming or presence of the Spirit without reference to tongues (Acts 4:31, 7:55, 9:17, 13:52).

(3) Instead of teaching that every Christian should expect to speak in tongues and that something is lacking in his spiritual life without tongues, Scripture teaches the opposite. Paul states expressly that every Christian has the Spirit (I Cor. 12:13), that only some have the gift of tongues (I Cor. 12:10), and that no one should feel inferior because he does not have any particular gift (I Cor. 12:15,16). Not everyone should expect to speak in tongues any more than he should expect to be an apostle (I Cor. 12:29,30). In the face of Paul's statements ("we . . . were all made to drink of one Spirit" and "do all speak in tongues?") it cannot be maintained that speaking in tongues is a necessary evidence of the full reception of the Spirit or that only those who speak in tongues have the Spirit.

Since the modern tongues movement is founded on such a thoroughly non-Biblical basis, how can one expect the tongues which result to be genuine? If the base is wrong, can the experience built on it be valid?

The Nature of Modern Tongues

Pentecostalism at first saw tongues as a gift to be used in missionary work. Charles Parham, the originator of the distinctive Pentecostal emphasis on tongues as initial evidence, taught that missionaries would no longer need to learn foreign languages.[1] Once they received the gifts of tongues they could go anywhere in the world and preach to the people in their own language. In the early days of the Pentecostal revival in Los Angeles it was reported that a woman named Anna Hall had gone to a Russian church in the city and preached to them in Russian, a language she had never studied.[2] A. G. Garr, known as the first Pentecostal foreign missionary, accepted all this. He went to India believing he could communicate with the people in his "tongue." The Pentecostal Synan reports what happened:

> The first white man to receive the experience at Azusa was one A. G. Garr, pastor of a holiness mission in Los Angeles. After his "baptism," Garr and his wife went to India where they expected to preach to the natives in their own languages. However, when this was attempted, it ended in failure. After their fiasco in India the Garrs traveled to Hong Kong where they set up a mission and learned Chinese in the more conventional manner. This was the outstanding attempt at carrying out Parham's

teaching concerning the missionary use of tongues, and it ended in failure.[3]

Pentecostals today see glossolalia primarily as a special prayer language which "bypasses the mind" and is not understood by the speaker.[4] The Neo-Pentecostal Bennett says that "speaking in tongues enables a person to speak or pray to God without interference from any human source, including himself; without the mind or emotions or will intruding into the picture."[5] At times, Pentecostals contend, the gift enables a person to communicate a needed message to someone whose language he does not know.[6] They maintain that glossolalia is real language, but it may be an "ancient dialect" of Hawaiian,[7] an "untranslatable dialect" of Chinese,[8] or a "very old form of Arabic."[9]

John Kildahl, a psychologist who devoted ten years to a special study of tongues-speaking, concluded that "psychological regression" was a factor "inherent in the development of the glossolalia experience." He explains:

> By regression is meant a reversion to an earlier level of maturity, during which the rational, common-sense, ego-controlled way of relating to life is somehow diminished. It is perhaps more child-like, less critical, and generally more free-floating in its nature. The glossolalia experience was generally introduced under the mass pressures of a group or a crowd, or the atmosphere was contagious because of the leader's charisma. The neophytes' critical faculties were subdued.[10]

Unless one first comes to disparage the mind and to elevate experience in his approach to God, contrary to Paul's admonition (I Cor. 14:20: "be not children in mind . . . in mind be men"), glossolalia cannot be induced.

Kildahl summarizes his findings about glossolalia in this way:

> Tongue-speaking does not look very uniquely spiritual to me after many experiences of watching people teach other people how to speak in tongues. I have observed the same routine everywhere I have been: (1) a meeting devoted to intense concentration on tongue-speaking, followed by (2) an atmosphere of heightened suggestibility to the words of the tongue-speaking leader, after which (3) the initiate is able to make the sounds he is instructed to make. It is the same procedure that a competent hypnotist employs.[11]

John Sherrill's description of the way he received the tongues experience fits Kildahl's analysis almost exactly. He had studied Pentecostalism sympathetically for a considerable time, coming to his study already convinced that Christianity could not be approached with the mind, but only through experience. Sherrill

111

himself recognizes that this new conviction of his was the "key" to his experience of tongues.[12] The day began with a Full Gospel Business Men's prayer breakfast which lasted for four hours. The atmosphere was emotionally charged; marvelous events occurred and marvelous experiences were related. After the meeting, as is customary, the large gathering broke up into smaller groups. Sherrill and his wife went up to a hotel room with five people who had had the tongues experience. After a short period in which the events of the morning were discussed, Sherrill's wife left the room. Her leaving was symbolic—the removal of the last vestige of objectivity. This removal of objectivity was essential to his having the experience. "She was deliberately taking with her our burden of objectivity. She was making it possible for me to step inside an experience, taking defenses out the door with her."[13]

As if he were being hypnotized, he began to lose his "own identity . . . until self-awareness disappeared."[14] The people in the room rose and formed a circle around him. "It was almost as if they were forming with their bodies a funnel through which was concentrated the flow of the Spirit that was pulsing through the room. It flowed into me as I sat there, listening to the Spirit-song around me."[15] "The very nature of that hour," he says, "was pure experience, with a maximum of allowing to happen what was going to happen, and a minimum of analysis."[16] What is "pure experience"? It means experience without thought, without examination or analysis; it "bypasses the mind."

If Paul's insistence on rationality and intelligibility were observed, Pentecostalism would dry up. Enthusiasm for the experience would wither, because to seek it one first has to lay aside his mind. Instead of being a fresh moving of the Spirit of God, Neo-Pentecostalism is seen to be only one more accommodation to the spirit of the age with its non-rationality, pragmatism, and orientation to experience.

Glossolalia, its advocates maintain, is superior to the normal language of prayer precisely because it does not involve the mind. "What blessing can it be," asks Christenson, "to pray when you have no idea what you are praying about?" And he answers: "Actually this is one of its greatest blessings—the fact that it is not subject to the limitations of your human intellect."[17] We ought to have serious questions about that. How can one even know he is praying to God if he is not using his mind? How can he be sure he is blessing God? Once I asked a tongues-speaker: "Since you do not know what you are saying, how can you be sure you are not saying, 'Jesus is anathema' " (I Cor. 12:3)?

He answered: "I would not consider that for a moment." But should he not really consider it?

Jesus taught us to pray thoughtfully and meaningfully. "And in praying use not vain repetitions, as the Gentiles do: for they think that they shall be heard for their much speaking" (Matt. 6:7). To "use vain repetitions" is a translation of *battalogeo*. *Batta* is onomatopoeia (formation of words in imitation of sounds, e.g. "buzz," "hiss"). *Bata* has no meaning; it is only sound (hence "*bata*-speaking").

After his caution against thoughtless and meaningless words Jesus gives an example of true prayer (vv. 9-13). One cannot pray in the manner this model teaches without vigorous mental effort and concentration. Imitating the model of Jesus will not permit us to abandon a vital part of our being but requires the whole person to participate. Jesus does not want simply to have God the Spirit, as a substitute for us, praying to God, or to have us made puppets by the Spirit, but he wants the prayers of real human beings offered to God. There is no place for quietism in prayer. When one consciously comes before God, humbled with a knowledge of his own need and God's greatness, and struggles to express his adoration and need to God, he is praying as Jesus taught. This is spiritual reality.

Are Modern Tongues Real Languages?

Kildahl's extensive research led him to the conclusion that "the evidence indicates that tongue-speech is not a language spoken anywhere in the world."[18] Though glossolalia may sound like a foreign language because of the rhythm, fluency, and feeling with which it is being uttered, it lacks rational content. "In spite of superficial similarities, glossolalia is fundamentally *not* language."[19] There are numerous reports that people have heard glossolalia and recognized a foreign language spoken, but "any time one attempts to verify them he finds that the stories have been greatly distorted or that the 'witnesses' turn out to be incompetent or unreliable from a linguistic point of view."[20] There is no reliable evidence that glossolalia is anything but nonsense sounds in imitation of language. "Of the hundreds of thousands of occasions on which glossolalia has been uttered, there is no tape recording that can be translated from a language spoken somewhere in the world. . . . If glossolalic utterances were somehow real languages, it would seem that there would exist somewhere in the world evidence that the speaking in tongues was in fact such a foreign language."[21]

How would a glossolalist answer this? Dennis Bennett's answer essentially is that asking for this kind of evidence would be like trying to put God into a test tube and God does not want to be put into a test tube. He derides those who come with their tape recorders looking for objective evidence and complains that people will not simply accept the testimony of those who have spoken in tongues or heard them spoken.[22] However, people can be mistaken,

and it is possible to get testimonials for anything (cf. Acts 8:10).
Bennett explains why he thinks it is impossible to get a tape
recording that can be translated.

> After all, objective investigation of a subjective experience
> has its limitations. Man, like God, is not an object but a
> subject and ultimately can be understood only by self-
> revelation, his willingness to tell what he is experiencing
> from within. . . . If a scientist desires to know what apple
> pie tastes like—what is the subjective experience of human
> beings eating apple pie—he or she can set up any number
> of experiments in which persons are observed eating pie
> and their reactions clocked and chronicled. Ultimately,
> however, the scientist might be well advised to taste a piece
> of pie. He might learn more from that than from years of
> investigation of others.[23]

Bennett has misconceived the nature of the question. We are not
asking about the subjective experience of a person claiming to
speak in tongues or how tongues-speaking makes one feel. Take his
apple pie illustration. He says if you want to know what apple pie
tastes like, taste it. Do not just observe people eating it. But we are
not asking how apple pie tastes. What we are asking is, Is there an
apple pie at all? Our situation is like this: someone says, "I have
eaten this pie, and it is delicious. You try it." When we look,
however, we do not see any pie. We try to take a picture of it, and
the print comes back blank. Similarly, some tell us, "God gave us
ability to speak language we have never learned, and it makes us
feel wonderful." We are not questioning whether he feels well (If
we want to know this, we would have to ask him) but whether he is
speaking real languages. To decide this we need hard evidence.

Modern Interpretation of Tongues

If the tongues spoken today are real languages, then those with
the gift of interpretation should be able to agree about their
meaning. To test this matter of interpretation Kildahl played
examples of tape-recorded glossolalia for several people who
claimed to have the gift of interpretation. He found that "in no
instance was there any similarity in the several interpretations given
by the interpreters who claimed to do a literal translation of the
tongue-speech."[24] One interpreter said a certain example of
glossolalia meant that the speaker was asking for help in deciding
whether to accept the offer of a new job. Another said the speaker
was giving thanks because he had recovered from a grave illness.
The interpreters were then confronted with the fact that they had
given different interpretations to the same tongue-speech. Without
batting an eye they said that God had given them different

interpretations of the same speech. The tongue-speaker himself, as is usual, said he did not know what it meant.[25] To attribute the contradictory interpretations to God is a serious matter. It is impossible that God should be the source of confusion (I Cor. 14:33).

Another example gives further insight into the nature of the interpretation of tongues. A missionary's son brought up in Africa decided to test the gift of interpretation. At a tongues-speaking meeting he repeated the Lord's prayer in the African dialect he had learned in his youth. When he finished, an interpreter said the meaning was that Christ would soon return.[26]

A similar case involves a Nigerian student who reported the following incident to me. On a visit to a neighboring state he met an interpreter of tongues. Okon asked the interpreter to give him the meaning of what he said. He then quoted Joel 2:28 in his native Ibo. The interpreter said he had spoken nonsense.

Pat Boone says of his wife's gift of tongues: "My wife was praising the Lord—in Latin. I knew she had never had a day of Latin. . . . Yet now she was saying very distinctly, 'Ava Diem! Ava Diem! Ava Diem!' or *"Praise God"* in a language she'd never learned. . . . We knew we'd just experienced a miracle. The Holy Spirit had given Shirley a phrase that He knew I could interpret, and for our mutual faith and edification."[27] *Ava* is a Latin word, but it means "grandmother"! Perhaps *ave* was meant instead of *ava*, but *ave* is a term of greeting or an expression of goodwill meaning "hail" or "farewell." *Diem* means "day." "Praise God" would be *lauda* (or *laudate*) *Deum*.

Can Modern Glossolalia Demonstrate the Coming of the Spirit?

Linguistic analysis shows that glossolalia is not a "supernatural phenomenon."[28] It is pseudolanguage made up of mere sounds put together without meaning and imitating the rhythm of real language. It is playing with language sounds as is done in bebop jazz, magical incantations, and the "pretend-language" of children and the chants in their games.[29] "Anybody can produce glossolalia if he is uninhibited and if he discovers what the 'trick' is."[30] The "trick" of playing with sounds is as simple as in this chant used by children:

> Acka, bacca, soda cracka,
> Acka, backa, boo.
> If your father chews tobacca,
> Out goes YOU.[31]

The practice of glossolalia by people with obviously heretical or even non-Christian beliefs is distressing and puzzling to many Pentecostals and Neo-Pentecostals. Ray Hughes, a traditional

Pentecostal, the general overseer of the Church of God (Cleveland, Tennessee), says: "Some who profess an experience of glossolalia do not subscribe to the tenets of Christianity. In fact, religious movements through the centuries, even the Satanists, have had their so-called glossolalia."[32] Christadelphians, who do not believe in the Trinity or the pre-existence of Christ, Mormons, Catholics, liberals, Hindus, and, as Hughes says, even Satanists speak in "tongues." Their gossolalia cannot be distinguished linguistically. In view of this fact how can glossolalia be an evidence that one has received the Holy Spirit?

On that point Hughes says: "A valid experience (the key word in this sentence is *valid*) of speaking in other tongues as the Spirit gives the utterance is evidence that God has control of one's life and that one is yielded to him."[33] He is saying that it is not just the speaking in tongues which is evidence of the Holy Spirit, but it must be a "valid experience." If anyone is thinking for a moment, he knows this introduces great problems into the whole Pentecostal conception. What is a "valid experience" of speaking in tongues? What are the criteria? How could we know there was a valid experience? Would the "tongue" have to be a real language with which the person had no acquaintance before? Would the test be a change of life? Hughes' statement (whatever the criteria laid down) means that one has to determine whether tongues-speaking is valid before he can say it indicates the presence of God's Spirit. The experience itself does not indicate it. This gives up the whole case.

Questions and Answers

1. What is the meaning of Mark 16:17?

"New tongues" are only one of five "signs" named in Mark 16:17,18. If one insists on speaking in tongues today because of this passage, he must also take up serpents and drink deadly poisons. The snake handling people are right in this regard. The passage does not say that the signs would follow every believer but the body of believers as a whole ("them that believe"). Acts shows the fulfillment of this when it records miracles performed only by apostles (2:43) and those upon whom the apostles laid hands (6:8, 8:5-6). The purpose of the signs was to confirm the word (Mk. 16:20) and not to give evidence of their "baptism in the Holy Spirit" or any other deeper experience. Note that the Spirit is not even mentioned in the context.

2. What is the significance of the verse, "Forbid not to speak with tongues" (I Cor. 14:39)?

First, it shows that the tongues discussed in I Corinthians 12-13

116

were a genuine gift. Those tongues conveyed genuine spiritual content and were capable of being translated (I Cor. 14:5. The root used here, *hermeneuein*, is employed in the New Testament to mean the translation of foreign languages: e.g. John 1:38, 41, 42, Mk. 5:41, 7:34, 15:22, 34, Mt. 1:23, Acts 9:36). Because of problems arising over the misuse of tongues, some in Corinth probably were trying to suppress them altogether. Paul indicates that they were neither to be sought nor forbidden.

Second, we are not forbidding people to do what Paul permitted when we try to dissuade them from the practice of glossolalia. Unlike the tongues Paul meant, present-day tongues-speaking has no content. The "gifts" are not the same. Instead of forbidding people to exercise a genuine gift, we are trying to persuade them not to engage in self-delusion.

Questions to Guide Study

1. What is the basis of the modern tongues movement? If the basis is insubstantial, can the experience be valid?
2. What three books in the New Testament mention tongues-speaking?
3. What is the "key" to John Sherrill's experience of tongues?
4. Do you believe it is possible to pray as Jesus taught in the model prayer while bypassing the mind?
5. Can the testimonials of tongue-speakers be regarded as sufficient evidence that real languages are being spoken?
6. Do you think that if the interpretation of tongues is a real gift of the Spirit, interpretations of the same tongue-speaking should agree? Why?
7. Do you see a problem for Pentecostalism in the fact that non-Christians use glossolalia?

---

[1] Vinson Synan, *The Holiness Pentecostal Movement in the United States,* pp. 102-103.

[2] Ibid., p. 110.

[3] Ibid., p. 111.

[4] Larry Christenson, Speaking in Tongues, cited in *The Holy Spirit in Today's Church,* ed. Erling Jorstad, pp. 87-88.

[5] Dennis J. Bennett, "The Gifts of the Holy Spirit," *The Charismatic Movement,* ed. Michael P. Hamilton (Grand Rapids: Eerdmans, 1975), p. 23.

[6] Ibid., p. 20.

[7] Ibid., p. 22.

[8] Ibid., p. 29.

[9] John Sherrill, *They Speak with Other Tongues,* p. 20.

[10] John Kildahl, *The Psychology of Speaking in Tongues* (New York: Harper and Row, 1972), p. 59.

[11] Ibid., p. 74.

[12] Sherrill, p. 9.

[13] Ibid., p. 120.
[14] Ibid., p. 121.
[15] Ibid., p. 122.
[16] Ibid.
[17] Christenson, cited in Jorstad, p. 88.
[18] John Kildahl, "Psychological Observations," *The Charismatic Movement,* p. 138.
[19] William J. Samarin, *Tongues of Men and Angels: The Religious Language of Pentecostalism* (New York: Macmillan, 1972), p. 227.
[20] Ibid., pp. 112-113.
[21] Kildahl, "Psychological Observations," p. 138.
[22] Bennett, p. 29.
[23] Ibid., p. 30.
[24] Kildahl, "Psychological Observations," p. 136.
[25] Ibid.
[26] Ibid., p. 137.
[27] Pat Boone, *A New Song* (Carol Stream, Ill.: Creation House, 1970), p. 118.
[28] Samarin, p. 227.
[29] Ibid., pp. 129-149.
[30] Ibid., pp. 227-228.
[31] Ibid., p. 147.
[32] Ray Hughes, "A Traditional Pentecostal Looks at the New Pentecostals," *Christianity Today,* XVIII (June 1974). 8.
[33] Ibid., p. 9.

CHAPTER XIII

What About Modern Miracles?

The charismatic movement assumes that miracles should be a normal part of the Christian's life. In fact, by definition, it holds that every Christian should receive miraculous manifestations of the Spirit. The miracles are usually "small things," says Dennis Bennett, and a "common miracle" is finding a "parking place when needed." "But, he affirms, "of course the big miracles still happen too."[1] The Full Gospel Business Men's Fellowship in its regular meetings features stories of the miraculous, and people feed hungrily on them.

At such a meeting in Gadsden, Alabama, evangelist Ken Cantrell claimed to have been involved in a stupendous miracle. The account of his speech in the *Gadsden Times* ("Miracle of the Fiery Furnace" by *Times* staff writer George Butler) calls it "one of the most amazing miracles of this century." The miracle supposedly occurred on August 7, 1953 to Cantrell, an Alabama sailor aboard the aircraft carrier the *USS Lake Champlain* near the Rock of Gibraltar. Cantrell was serving in the catapult room of the carrier with a crew of fifteen others. Suddenly there was an explosion and fire. Fifteen of the crew were killed instantly. Only Cantrell survived. When doctors examined him later, they found no burns, "not even a singed hair, not even a smell of smoke about his body."

Cantrell had been fasting for seventeen days and "engrossed in Brother Franklin Hall's book, 'Because of your Unbelief.' By this time, I had studied the book so much that I had it almost memorized. It seemed that I just could not doubt God anymore. My faith in Him as a complete Savior against any harm and against any trouble, obstacle or danger was made secure." Note the idea, inherent in perfectionistic thought, that he had reached the point of *total* or *absolute* faith. When such a point is reached, the perfectionist believes one can look for spectacular things to happen.

This is the way Cantrell related what happened:

> At 10:55 a.m., the crew began coming back into the room. By 11:02 every one of the 16 was back in the room. We were ready for our duties.
> At 11:03 a.m., someone above us had made a blunder.

119

The hightest gasoline that was pouring into our room was now a huge sheet of billowing flames. . . .

Horror came over their faces. Some tried to run. Many were screaming "Fire, Fire." I also yelled "Fire." Huge billows of raging flames were rushing toward everyone. It came fast.

It was like lightning. As flames of death engulfed one by one and many at one time, my eyes seemed to have supernatural eyesight. I could look and even see through the flames.

By fasting, Jesus had clothed me with the power of the Holy Ghost fire. This supernatural power . . . was upon all of my body . . .

The flames were around Joe [Carnes, his friend] and around me. I was immune to them . . . I could not feel any natural heat whatsoever. The flames were getting bigger and the smoke was going upward through ventilation areas through the deck.

I was stunned and amazed but I was not afraid. I wanted to help my friend. Soon, however, I could smell the flesh of human bodies cooking. I could hear the frying of flesh. . . . It just did not seem possible that I could be alive in that furnace of fire.

He picked up the body of his friend, Joe, and started to take him out. He was reluctant to touch the red-hot door.

The Lord told me: "Be not afraid, grab the wrench, open the door and walk out." I got closer to the door and hesitated. Again the Lord said: "Be not afraid, I am with you. You shall not die. Open the door and walk out."

I still held the corpse of Joe. I picked up the red-hot wrench with my right bare hand and used it to open the hatch. I walked out in front of the amazed and bewildered officers, chaplain and spectators.

I laid the remains of Joe on the deck outside. By this time, the flesh had come off some of his bones. . . . I returned, against the orders of officers, and picked up another one of my buddies. His flesh also was burned until it fell from his bones.

The skulls were shrunken to about one-half their size. This was true for each and every one of the bodies. I carried them all out, one by one, and laid them down.

On his last visit he got the book *Because of Your Unbelief.* "Other books all around had been burned to ashes, but that particular book was not even singed." Butler reports that the "surviving sailor was summoned to sick bay for examination by doctors. In the sick bay, a strange thing happened. There were sailors there for treatment. As he walked by, each person was healed instantly and left the room."

Evaluation of the Report

What shall we say about such an account? Should we simply accept it? Perhaps Cantrell embellished a true account of a narrow escape. How could we go about investigating it? A letter of inquiry received the following reply from (Mrs.) S. R. Morrison (Head, Research and Public Inquiries Branch, Office of Information, Department of the Navy, Washington, D.C., dated April 6, 1972):

> In regard to Mr. Ken Cantrell and events alleged to have occurred on USS LAKE CHAMPLAIN on August 7, 1953, a thorough investigation of the ship's records, including the deck log, has been carried out by personnel in the Ship's Histories Section of the Division of Naval History. A number of discrepancies in Mr. Cantrell's heroic tale are evident.
>
> LAKE CHAMPLAIN'S log discloses no disastrous fire of any kind on or about August 7, 1953. The vessel did have a gasoline fire in July, 1957, while in Marseille, France, during the unloading of automobiles onto a lighter alongside. The fire started on the lighter, not the carrier, and spread from the ship's stern, not her bow. Three of LAKE CHAMPLAIN'S men were killed on the lighter and five injured. The entire event, occurring four years after Mr. Cantrell's account, with but three fatalities and at the opposite end of the ship, scarcely resembles the Cantrell story.
>
> Bureau of Naval Personnel records show that Mr. Cantrell was detached April 26, 1953, and was transferred to the Naval Receiving Station, Philadelphia, Pennsylvania. No record exists to show any subsequent return to the ship.

Three facts are to be noted. (1) The ship was not located in the area where Cantrell said it was. This could be overlooked, however, if the other information were correct. (2) There was no fire of the kind Cantrell described. (3) When there was a fire (different in nature and date from Cantrell's story), Cantrell was not even on the ship. This case is typical. When one begins to investigate a reported miracle, the evidence seems to disappear before one's eyes.

Such fantastic stories, to which people eagerly listen, are an illustration of what we have called "charisma-mania"—the thirst to tell and to hear the marvelous. It was this preoccupation with the miraculous which gave rise to the apocryphal gospels and acts. In these works the marvelous was introduced and cherished for its own sake and looked upon as being more powerful in bringing conviction than the word of God. Jesus found such an attitude in miracle-hungry people in his day. He did not regard it as a spiritually healthy outlook. "Then certain of the scribes and Pharisees answered him, saying, Teacher, we would see a sign from thee. But he answered and said unto them, An evil and adulterous generation seeketh after a sign; and there shall no sign be given to it but the sign of Jonah the prophet: for as Jonah was three days and three nights in the belly of the whale; so shall the Son of man be three days and three nights in the heart of the earth" (Matt. 12:38-40). There is one sign on which people should fix their attention. With it they should be content—the sign of Jesus' resurrection from the dead.

People then, as now, were sure that witnessing the spectacular would make faith and repentance easy. The rich man in hades made such an assumption. He asked that Lazarus be sent from the dead to his father's house and testify to his five brothers "lest they also come into this place of torment" (Lk. 16:27,28). Abraham answered, "They have Moses and the prophets; let them hear them" (v. 29). The rich man insisted, "Nay, father Abraham: but if one go to them from the dead, they will repent" (v. 30). With finality Abraham said: "If they hear not Moses and the prophets, neither will they be persuaded, if one rise from the dead" (v. 31). Though it is easy to assume that a miracle so great would compel someone to change, Jesus assures us that there is nothing more powerful than Scripture to bring men to repentance.

Scripture insists that we have been given enough evidence to lead us to faith and life. "Many other signs therefore did Jesus in the presence of the disciples, which are not written in this book: but these are written, that ye may believe that Jesus is the Christ, the Son of God; and that believing ye may have life in his name" (John 20:30,31). One cannot demand more evidence without demeaning the sufficient evidence that has already been given.

What Is a Miracle?

An intelligent discussion of miracles requires a careful definition of the term. Three words are used in the New Testament for miracle: *semeion,* "sign," *teras,* "wonder," and *dunamis,* "power." The Biblical concept of miracle includes the insights conveyed by each of these terms—that is, it takes all three Biblical terms to define a miracle. Every real miracle is at once a "sign," a "wonder," and a direct exertion of God's "power."

(1) *Semeion,* "sign," is the apostle John's favorite word for miracle. It indicates that a miracle points to something beyond

itself, does not exist for its own sake. It is a means of teaching. "Sign" stresses the fact that a miracle has meaning or "significance" and is not a random occurrence.

In John 6:1-14 we have the account of Jesus' feeding five thousand (called a "sign" in verse 14). In this context and in direct connection with this miracle Jesus says: "I am the bread of life: he that cometh to me shall not hunger, and he that believeth on me shall never thirst" (John 6:35). People should have observed the miracle and said: "This is what it means: Jesus Christ is the bread of life. He is the one who satisfies the deepest needs human beings have. We will be sustained by him." Instead, they wrongly centered their attention on the miracle itself and wanted it repeated.

John 9:1-8 records the "sign" of Jesus' healing the man born blind. The meaning of this miracle, Jesus explains, is that he is "the light of the world" (John 9:5). A person who witnessed this miracle should have realized that Jesus indeed is the source of all the light there is in the world.

John 11 gives the account of Jesus' raising Lazarus from the dead. Jesus' explanation of this "sign" is: "I am the resurrection, and the life: he that believeth on me, though he die, yet shall he live" (John 11:25). The purpose of this miracle, and indeed of every miracle of Christ, was to teach people who he is and to fix their attention on him rather than on the miracle as merely a spectacular and exciting event.

(2) *Teras* is a "wonder." The equivalent of this word in Latin is *miraculum,* which means "a strange thing," a "thing which excites wonder," from *miror,* "to wonder," or "be amazed." It is from *miraculum* that we get our word "miracle." By definition a "miracle" is unusual. It fills with wonder precisely because it is an extraordinary, unexpected event. A miracle is never the norm. This is contrary to the belief of some people, who think that when one becomes a Christian, he should witness miracles every day. But miracles have never been ordinary occurrences; they could not have been and retained their character as miracles.

There are two ways to destroy the Biblical miracles. The first way is to deny them outright or to rationalize them, as the liberal does. The second, more effective way is to make everything a miracle. For example, if I were to say that the rising of the sun in the East is a miracle, what would it be if it rose some morning in the West? If I say every birth is a miracle, what then is the virgin birth of Christ? Was not the conception of Christ different from all other conceptions? Is it not that difference which makes it a miracle? If I make everything a miracle, remove the unusual element from it, I have destroyed miracle as a unique category.

(3) *Dunamis* means "power." It is translated as "mighty work" or "mighty deed." How is the exertion of God's power a miracle since everything is ultimately caused, preserved, or permitted by the

123

power of God? God works through secondary causes in preserving and sustaining creation, but a miracle is the direct exertion of his power. It is a result produced by the immediate power of God. The exertion of God's power is immediate in two senses. It does not involve time or means. For instance, the multiplying of the loaves and fishes (John 6:1-14) is a miracle. God is continually multiplying loaves and fishes, is he not? When the wheat is planted, does it not germinate and grow by the power of God? And do not fish reproduce by the power of God? Why then is it a miracle when Jesus multiplied the loaves and fishes? It is a miracle because this was an immediate exertion of God's power. He did not use means and time.

Sometimes we are told that every prayer expects a miracle. If we ask God to act at all, we are told, we are asking him to perform a miracle. No, not if we understand what a miracle is. God can work in ways other than through a miracle. He can work through secondary causes, and that is the way he has usually worked. In extraordinary situations, for good and sufficient reasons, God has put forth his power directly.

We are taught to pray, "Give us this day our daily bread." If I plow my garden, cut the grass and weeds, gather the fruit and vegetables, prepare them for eating, do you think I have anything to thank God for? Has he not caused them to grow? Is he not responsible for the life in the seed in the first place? When I pray for God to give me a good harvest, is it inconsistent for me to cultivate the garden? Of course not, because I expect God to work through means. In the absence of a specific promise of a miracle, I should expect God to use means, and I should make use of the means God has ordained. This does not mean that I have removed God from the universe or that I do not understand God is active in the world or that I exclude the benefits that come from prayer. It means only a recognition of the difference between miracle and God's providential working (the difference between his work of creation and his work of preservation in the universe, Neh. 9:6).

It makes a great practical difference whether one distinguishes God's providential or usual working from a miracle. If one expects a miracle, he waits for God alone to act. But if a person expects God to use means, he does not feel that he is acting in unbelief but in faith when he himself makes use of all the resources God has given, including medicine, surgery, hard work, and his own common sense.

In 1973 Wesley Parker, an eleven year old boy who lived in Barstow, California was supposedly cured of diabetes by a miraculous healer. His parents threw away his insulin. Very soon the boy went into a coma. They refused to give him insulin because they reasoned that it would show a lack of faith. Three days later, the boy died (August 22, 1973). The parents did not want to have him buried because they said the Lord would raise him. A day passed, then two, and three without his being raised. Finally they said the Lord would raise him on the fourth day as he did Lazarus. After the fourth day, they permitted him to be buried, but they did not attend the funeral because they still insisted the Lord would raise him. The parents were later tried and convicted of child abuse and involuntary manslaughter. The miraculous healer was not charged.

Tragedies like this, resulting from a misplaced confidence in miracle healers, are not infrequent. If the parents had not been misled by the healer's promise of a miracle, they could have expected to use means in promoting their son's health. They could have given him the insulin with thanksgiving to God, for the insulin was God's gift.

The miracles of the Bible are different from modern alleged miracles. One of the great differences is that the miracles of the Bible have a sufficient occasion, purpose, and rationale. That purpose or rationale is to attest the messenger of God. "Signs, and wonders and mighty works" were objective evidence that a person was an apostle (II Cor. 12:12, cf. Rom. 15:19). The miracles of the Bible cluster around great events. They are not spaced evenly throughout all periods of Biblical history. There are long periods without miracles. They cluster around events concerned with the development and revelation of God's plan of redemption. "Signs and wonders," "manifold powers," and "gifts of the Holy Spirit" were given to confirm or authenticate the word of the Lord (Heb. 2:3,4). Since God's revelation is complete in Christ, alleged miracles today lack the Biblical rationale. Belief that Scripture is complete and sufficient and belief that miraculous gifts have ceased are bound inextricably together.

Are There Miraculous Healings?

Dr. William Nolen investigated three individuals or groups who professed to be healers.[2] (1) Kathryn Kuhlman (who died in 1976 from complications following open heart surgery), the famous miracle healer, maintained that the Holy Spirit healed through her. (2) Norbu Chen (who is not Oriental but changed his name from Charles Vernon Alexander II) professes to heal by strange Tibetan powers which he says he learned in Sikkim. He claims to concentrate all the energy of his body to one point and then to release it for healing. (3) The "psychic surgeons" of the Philippines without using instruments or anesthetics claim to open bodies and remove diseased tissue and organs with their bare hands. Their "operations" cause no pain, leave no scars, and require no recovery time. Their operations are pure illusion. The "tissue" and "organs" they remove (and quickly dispose of) are really balls of cotton stained with red dye (sometimes the viscera of chickens).

These healers use different methods of healing and hold different beliefs. One of them (Norbu Chen) not only does not profess to be a Christian but is openly hostile to Christianity. Yet they all achieve about the same results. A disorder which one can heal (a functional disorder), they all can heal. A disease which one cannot heal (an organic disease), none can heal. Faith itself operating as a power in the mind of the patient, bringing relief from anxiety and hope of healing, effects the cure (of functional disorders only) or, at least, relieves the symptoms. This conclusion is required by the fact that the same results can be achieved regardless of the belief involved, whether it is the physician's placebo, the shaman's magic, or the faith healer's appeal to the Spirit.

Miraculous healers "do heal, in a certain sense. Kathryn Kuhlman 'cures' the pain of a backache, Norbu Chen stops a migraine, David Oligani [a psychic surgeon] gets rid of a patient's stomach ache."[3] "However, if a patient goes to the Philippines, to Kathryn Kuhlman or to any other healer for treatment of a serious organic disease—cancer of the rectum, for example, or a tuberculosis infection of the lung—that patient may well pay for his folly with his life. Tragically, this sort of thing happens every day."[4]

> Search the literature, as I have, and you will find no documented cures by healers of gallstones, heart disease, cancer or any other serious organic disease. Certainly, you'll find patients temporarily relieved of their upset stomachs, their chest pains, their breathing problems; and you will find healers, and believers, who will interpret this interruption of symptoms as evidence that the disease is cured. But when you track the patient down and find out what happened later, you always find the "cure" to have been purely symptomatic and transient. The underlying disease remains.[5]

How strong the power of suggestion can be is shown in certain societies which have faith in the powers of a witch doctor to curse and to heal. In such cultures people become severely ill and even die as a result of having a curse placed upon them or having their spirit stolen. The same people recover rapidly when the curse is removed by a stronger spell or the soul is believed to be returned.[6]

A physician had a faith healer try to cure three seriously ill patients without their knowledge of his efforts. He had no success. The physician then told the patients about the faith healer and led them to believe he could help them. Without the knowledge or participation of the faith healer, the physician told them the healer would be trying to cure them the next day. The healing was to be done without the healer's being present. This deliberate deception had dramatic results; the patients showed remarkable improvement. "These three patients were greatly helped by a belief that was false—that the faith healer was treating them from a distance—suggesting that 'expectant trust' in itself can be a powerful healing force."[7]

A patient of Dr. Nolen's lost her voice and could not speak above a whisper. The condition continued for four years. Examination determined that nothing was wrong with her vocal cords. There was no reason she should not be able to speak, but the patient could not accept this. She was actually punishing herself because she felt guilty about her husband's death. They had quarrelled shortly before he died in a traffic accident. It became necessary for Dr. Nolen to perform surgery to correct another problem. When he visited her after the surgery he decided to try an unorthodox treatment.

> "Louise," I said when I visited her the day after surgery, "when we operated on you we had to put a tube into your windpipe to give you the anesthetic. When we did that, I noticed your vocal cords were stuck together just a bit so I spread them apart. I bet that's why you've had to whisper all these years. By tomorrow I think your voice will be back to normal."
>
> Sure enough, when I made rounds the next day Louise was all smiles. She spoke to me in a perfectly normal voice. "It's wonderful, Dr. Nolen," she said. "Spreading those vocal cords did it. Thank you very much." . . .
>
> I didn't cure her by spreading her cords but after four years of mourning Louise was ready to forgive herself, and I gave her an excuse for getting her voice back . . . The medical literature is full of cures of hysterical symptoms like Louise's.[8]

The disorders "cured" by miracle healers are like Louise's. "It is in treating patients of this sort that healers claim their most dramatic triumphs."[9]

Provision has been made for our perfect healing. But perfect healing does not belong to this life, as many Biblical facts make clear: Paul's "thorn in the flesh" (II Cor. 12:7-10), Trophimus' being left at Miletus sick (II Tim. 4:20), Paul's recommendations to Timothy for treatment of his "often infirmities" (I Tim. 5:23). Those who think the Christian should here and now be free from sickness make the same mistake as the perfectionists: they misconceive the nature of Christian existence (see Acts 14:22, Rom. 8:18-23). Perfect health, like perfect holiness, will be given at our glorification, when the last enemy, death, is abolished (I Cor. 15:26) and we receive the redemption of our body (Rom. 8:23), and stand before God in a body transformed and made like Christ's

(Phil. 3:21). To demand to have perfect health now is to fail to respect God's order of salvation.

Questions to Guide Study

1. Does it make any practical difference whether there is any difference between a miracle and the providential working of God?
2. If people could witness miracles, would faith and repentance necessarily be made easier?
3. What is the difference between a functional and an organic disorder? Is there a difference in the way they can be cured?
4. What are the implications for the meaning of miracle in the Biblical terms "sign," "wonder," and "power"?
5. What is the rationale of Biblical miracles?
6. Is it true that every prayer asks for a miracle?
7. Is the Christian promised perfect health in this life?

---

¹ Dennis Bennett, "The Gifts of the Holy Spirit," p. 17.
² William A. Nolen, *Healing: A Doctor in Search of a Miracle* (New York: Random House, 1974).
³ Ibid., p. 275.
⁴ Ibid., pp. 307-308.
⁵ Ibid., p. 293.
⁶ Jerome D. Frank, *Persuasion and Healing: A Comparative Study of Psychotherapy* (Baltimore: Johns Hopkins Press, 1961), pp. 39-42.
⁷ Ibid., pp. 60-61.
⁸ Nolen, pp. 285-286.
⁹ Ibid., p. 287.